THE SERIOUS GUIDE TO
JOKE WRITING

THE SERIOUS GUIDE TO

JOKE WRITING

SALLY HOLLOWAY

bookshaker

First Published in Great Britain 2010
by www.BookShaker.com

To Steve, for all the jokes we've shared and all those yet to come.

PRAISE

"This is the best book about joke writing that I have ever read (and I've read a lot!). The exercises that she sets out in each chapter are incredibly easy to grasp and indicate a clear method without in any way handicapping the individual performer's creativity. Sally has written a very concise and accessible book that deserves to be on the bookshelf of every beginner comic and every seasoned professional. I wish it had existed when I started out."
Logan Murray, author of 'Be a Great Standup'

"I really wish I'd had this book when I was starting out as a writer. Then I'd have had a time machine as well!"
Wayne Kline, US network TV writer

"Sally enables you to find what is funny about a subject and extract it to paper in your own unique way. The whole course has been very helpful in tooling me up for when I get stuck writing jokes."

"This course has exceeded my expectations. I enjoyed the exercises, especially joke-webs. I like how they could take you quite a distance away from the original subject without trying too hard."

"I loved the surrealist inquisition it really helped to generate ideas away from the obvious."

"Since your course, I can't stop writing redefinitions!"

"I loved the surrealist Inquisition and stream of consciousness ways of writing because it loosens and frees associations and get the sub-conscious flowing creatively."

"I just wanted to say how much I enjoyed the course, thank you very much Sally, it has done wonders for me."

"Writing jokes from Newspapers has created a revolution in my brain – thank you, I have never felt so creative."

Feedback from students on Sally's Joke Writing Classes

ACKNOWLEDGEMENTS

This book has been written over two years.

When I talk about 'the class' I actually mean a number of classes I have taught over that time and I'm very grateful to all of the participants.

Amused Moose Comedy Writing classes (2004, 2005, 2006) were my early guinea pigs along with the 2007 'Jokes Jokes Jokes' class held in Hastings.

Paul F. Taylor, Ayad Andrews, Kim Dolman, Maureen Younger Isabelle Tonge, Christine Lawrence, David the mystery man from Hastings, Paul Westwood, Kevin Conn, Sue Lenier, John Kelly, Bea Lacey, Steve Savage, Martin Ansell, Val Lee, Karl Edrik (RIP, he's out there somewhere enjoying the cosmic joke) and Steve Rose from my two 2008 Joke writing Classes. These good people sparked the whole idea of a joke writing book.

Jennifer Allen, Danny Banks, Karl Davison, Anton Hammond, Kara Jeffrey, Bruce Knight, Bea Lacey, Val Lee, Sue Lenier, Clive Osborne, Kaye Quinley and Steve Savage from the 2008 Stand-up Course. They created the *Strikes Joke-web* in Chapter 3.

Heather Alexandra, Martin Ansell, Simon Cooper, LouLou Cousin, Karl Davison, Jean Kelley, Anton Hammond, Anita Jardine, Val Lee, Sidonie Mitchel Wade, Clive Osbourne, Suzi Payton and Steve Savage from the 2009 Intermediate Stand-up Class. They did the *Art-Relationships Double Joke-web* in Chapter 5.

Thanks also to the 2008 Amused Moose, Edinburgh Comedy Writing Course as well as the people who attended my workshop at the 2008 British Association of Comedy Writers Conference which the Carol Vorderman exercise in *Writing Jokes From Newspapers* (Chapter 7) is based on.

I'd like to give a particular mention to...

Elisa Roche from the Daily Express who kindly gave me permission to use her article 'It's sum task to find a new Carol' in *Writing Jokes From Newspapers* (Chapter 7).

Paul Westwood, Sue Lenier and John Kelly (2008 Joke writing Class) who wrote nearly all the jokes in *Redefinitions - How Did The Class Do* (Chapter 1).

LouLou Cousin and Jean Kelley (2009 Intermediate Stand-up course) who gave me permission to use their homework and wrote the bulk of the jokes in *Hadron Joke Collider - How Did The Class Do* (Chapter 5).

Piers Campbell (Amused Moose Comedy Writing Course) who wrote the Mohican story in one of my early classes and I have used it as an example ever since. It appears in Chapter 1.

Bea Lacey (2008 Joke Writing Course) for showing me that the Surrealist Inquisition was a viable method of joke writing and for some people it's where it's at!

Ayad Andrews and Sue Lenier who wrote various jokes featured in several *How Did the Class Do* sections. Ayad also read the mostly terrible early drafts of this book and gave me encouragement anyway.

Angie McAvoy from whose writing method I developed the Stream-of-Consciousness exercises.

Andrew Jobbins who experimented on jokes with me in the late nineties and with whom I discovered that jokes exist in the ether.

Hils Jago for knowing I could teach joke writing before I knew it myself.

Simon Dowd who is the comic who used to write toppers for my sketches (Chapter 8), and whose Friday afternoon phone calls (Chapter 13) made me reassess what comedy was all about. He gave me endless support writing this book.

Rachel Spring and John Kelly who, along with Paul Westwood (already mentioned above), proof read this book at different stages.

The Illiterati. My local creative writing group who allowed me to read them sections of this book (sometimes over and over again).

Andrea Samuelson for endless support and 'power chats'.

Sue Middleton for being so supportive always.

Dan Evans, whose comments on my manuscript were so insightful that this book is better for him having read it.

Joe Gregory for redrawing my cartoons so wonderfully.

Steve Amos and SATC for kick-starting my comedy courses in Hastings.

Finally, I am very grateful to Tim Vine, Jason John Whitehead and Tiernan Dooyab for letting me use their beautifully crafted jokes as examples in this book.

CONTENTS

INTRODUCTION

THE DIFFERENCE BETWEEN BEING FUNNY WITH YOUR MATES AND WRITING JOKES FOR A LIVING

'Who here is funny with their mates?' I always ask my new classes.

A few people always sheepishly put their hand up.

'Don't be shy,' I say. 'Because if you're funny with your mates you can transfer that skill to doing it for a living. You really can.'

People start to look very pleased at this point.

'BUT,' I warn them, 'you're going to have to put some work in.'

One of the biggest challenges I face as a joke writing tutor is that people want to write jokes without putting in any effort because that's how it feels when they are being funny with their mates.

I would argue that when you're with mates you are actually working quite hard without realising it. It seems easy because you're relaxed, you're confident, you're going over a well worn subject you know and love. The general chit chat of the group gives you numerous potential set-up lines to play off, and even though you're thinking really hard in order to do that, you're enjoying it so much that you don't even notice how furiously your brain is working and how totally focused you are.

Now think of someone on a popular comedy show. Say Frankie Boyle when he was on *Mock the Week*. It looks like he's just sitting there riffing with rest of the panellists just like you do when you're with your mates but in fact he's been out the night before at a couple of gigs trying out this material in advance. In fact you can still listen to his podcasts of live recordings of him previewing the material in preparation for the show[1]. His big skill is that he makes it appear relaxed, spontaneous and conversational. It's deliberately made to look as casual as when you are being funny with your mates.

So how can you be as funny as Frankie Boyle or the writers on *Mock the Week?* Many people tell me that they find it difficult when they try to write jokes on their own. They tell me they've always wanted to be a comedy writer but when they finally have time to get on with it, they don't know what to do. They become anxious about whether they're really funny, and start making cups of tea, which turns into lunch, then they're on the phone to old friends and then they get out a comedy DVD (to give them inspiration!) but it just means they end up slumped in front of the telly and lack the will to try writing again. They don't need to tell me all this. I've done it myself. We all have.

This book is here to help you. For example, if you want to write jokes about the latest celebrity scandal, to write that subject down on a piece of

---

[1] See http://itunes.apple.com/us/podcast/frankie-boyle-mock-the-week/id323684930

paper, and look at it hoping for something to come, is to set yourself too big a target.

At Christmas when you are faced with an enormous turkey, you don't wonder how you are going eat it. You carve it up, pull it to pieces, chew it bit by bit, make a stew out of it the next day, boil the bones for stock and give the giblets to the dog. That's what we're going to do with our subjects: break them down, pull them apart, mentally chew them over bit by bit and come at it with our comedic knife (or cutting wit!) from different angles.

This book contains six different practical ways to write jokes, or six different ways to approach the turkey, plus some theories and advice to help you stay relaxed and focused just like you are when you're with your mates. These methodical writing exercises mimic the natural joke writing ability that most of us display at some time, and heighten awareness of joke structures. Once you have mastered the basics you will be able to write jokes about anything. Because, let's face it, if you spontaneously think of a gag it's usually on a subject that engages you on some level, even if it irritates the hell out of you; in fact more so because it will be niggling away at your brain cells until they respond with humour. So the second big difference between being funny with your mates and writing jokes at home is subject matter. Could your mates in the pub really write jokes on the latest BP Oil spill or the Japanese economy? That's where formal joke writing methods come in, and, believe me, it's really exciting to think of great jokes on a dull story and this book will show you how to put the time in to find them.

Yes, there's no getting away from that last point. I am going to ask you to do some work, but you will never have to stare at a blank piece of paper again. You will have things to do, associations to write out, links to find, angles to come from. Do this regularly, and you will train the joke writing muscles in your brain to become like a lean mean chess machine that knows all the moves and can work out every angle, every scenario, because jokes are there to be found and right now it's time to start looking for them.

HOW TO USE THIS BOOK

Ideally I'd like everyone to read every word of this book but I know in the real world that's not always possible. That's why it is divided into practical and theory chapters.

The practical chapters contain the actual joke writing methods that you can do whenever you want. I have created this flow chart to help you find your way around them. If you only have time to read one bit of theory, I recommend *What's Most Important: Time, Tenacity or Talent?* (Chapter 8), closely followed by *Background Processing* (Chapter 2). Or why not do the practical exercises when you have time to write and read the theory chapters in bed or on the train.

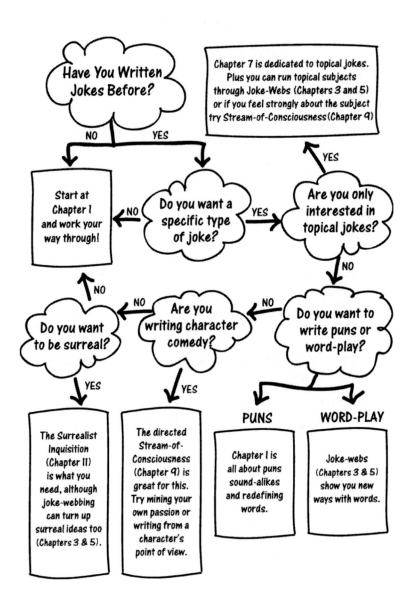

Have You Written Jokes Before?

NO → Start at Chapter 1 and work your way through!

YES → Do you want a specific type of joke?

Chapter 7 is dedicated to topical jokes. Plus you can run topical subjects through Joke-Webs (Chapters 3 and 5) or if you feel strongly about the subject try Stream-of-Consciousness (Chapter 9)

Do you want a specific type of joke?
NO → Start at Chapter 1 and work your way through!
YES → Are you only interested in topical jokes?

Are you only interested in topical jokes?
YES (up to the topical jokes box)
NO → Do you want to write puns or word-play?

Do you want to write puns or word-play?
NO → Are you writing character comedy?
PUNS → Chapter 1 is all about puns sound-alikes and redefining words.
WORD-PLAY → Joke-webs (Chapters 3 & 5) show you new ways with words.

Are you writing character comedy?
NO → Do you want to be surreal?
YES → The directed Stream-of-Consciousness (Chapter 9) is great for this. Try mining your own passion or writing from a character's point of view.

Do you want to be surreal?
NO → Do you want a specific type of joke?
YES → The Surrealist Inquisition (Chapter 11) is what you need, although joke-webbing can turn up surreal ideas too (Chapters 3 & 5).

WHO AM I TO TELL YOU HOW TO WRITE JOKES?

I sit at my office desk. I look like I'm happily writing jokes, but two minutes earlier – without any deliberate instruction from my brain – my body got up and headed towards the door. My conscious mind had to act quickly to interrupt it, tell it to sit down and carry on working. I do this once an hour. In a speeded-up video I'd look a baboon circling in its cage.

It's the late Nineties and tonight I'm due on a Radio 5 news-based panel show called *The Treatment*. They give me two days to write a two-minute witty piece on a topical subject of their choice. Boy, do they choose some hard subjects – the European Exchange Rate Mechanism and the Government's Poverty Report spring to mind. On top of that I have to think of funny asides about three other subjects and an opening 'highlight of the week' gag.

The only way for me to achieve this is to put in two 8 – 10 hour writing days. For a stand-up comic used to working 20 minutes a night, it's a bit of a shock, but I always manage it.

And while I'm managing it the analytical side of me notices my brain's own process of writing.

I know that if I work on a subject long enough I start to see all the different ways that words, sentences and phrases can be interpreted. Sometimes, though, this seems to take forever and looking back I realize that this is when I first started to look for ways to speed up the process, or quickly mimic my natural way of thinking.

I became aware of my emotional patterns too. When I started working on a subject I would always worry that there would be no jokes on it. The way to overcome this was to focus on my belief (that I now teach) that jokes are not genius thunderbolts, they already exist in the ether, and all I had to do was keep looking for them.

The second pattern I noticed was that at around 3pm on the afternoon of the recording (we used to record at 6.30) I would truly believe with all my heart that what I'd written was utter rubbish and that I was going to fail. A younger me would have gone into panic mode but I learnt to realize it was a mid-afternoon slump, to put the feelings to one side and keep working.

Basically the answer to all my problems was always to keep working, to keep sifting through ideas, to keep looking for that other angle or meaning or context. When I was exasperated with one subject I simply moved on to the next.

This brought me to my third discovery: no matter how much I thought I'd run out of ideas on a subject, if left it by taking a break or visiting another subject, when I returned to it my brain would have new ideas. I started to think of this as background processing – the same mechanism that a computer uses when you set it to print or search.

And now I teach that too.

As well as doing *The Treatment* every couple of months I got other radio work, always the 'funny things about the news' slots such as on LBC some

Sunday mornings. With each show, my joke writing methods developed and I started to wonder whether, if you had enough ways of looking at things, you could write jokes on anything. Admittedly they might not be the best jokes in the world, but if you are working on the economic outlook or the coverage of the Iraq war, finding a bit of humour is a glorious thing.

This was all doing wonders for my writing, but could I teach it to others? I got the chance to find out when a group of newish comics hired me to teach them topical joke writing. I was thrilled and eagerly lectured them for an hour and then gave them half an hour of practical exercises.

During that session people wrote jokes the way I'd shown them, which meant it could be taught (so many people say it can't). I was pleased when I was asked to go back and do it again, although the feedback was that they wanted less lecture and more practical next time – something I have adhered to in my teaching ever since. I also taught stand-up workshops at Jackson's Lane Community Centre in North London and started incorporating bits of joke writing into the classes.

Between 1999 – 2003, apart from doing radio and a bit of telly, I mainly toured round the worldwide comedy circuit: Amsterdam, Abu Dhabi, Paris, Kos, as well as numerous small towns across England, Ireland, Scotland and Wales. Nowadays, whenever anyone tells me where they come from I say, 'Oh I did a gig there, in the arts centre/a little pub on the high street. It was great/awful/really weird!'

I had to give up stand-up in 2003 due to ill-health, and the enforced rest gave me a lot of time to think. Once I'd done the inevitable soul-searching I found my analytical mind delving even more deeply into jokes. I thought about jokes I'd written, jokes I wished I'd written, and how to find jokes that had yet to be written but were out there. This got an outlet a year later in 2004 when I was invited to teach the first three weeks of the Amused Moose comedy writing course. It was nine hours of teaching, and all nine of them were to be devoted to writing jokes. Still not well, it was the only work I did that year. But it was ideal. I built the course on everything I'd learned: three basic joke writing methods, using newspapers as a basis for jokes, joke-webs (which are mind-maps® with a special adaptation to heighten joke writing) and Stream-of-Consciousness (where you write or talk about something you care about without stopping, for a set amount of time).

It was a bit rough round the edges. The more experienced students loved it but others struggled with some of the concepts. The feedback was that they'd like me to teach it again the next year but they wanted more explanation. I was happy to oblige. I started thinking of all jokes in relation to my courses, and to work out how I could teach people to write them.

My nine hours teaching the following year went even better. I broke each joke writing method down into easy-to-follow stages, and added direction to the Stream-of-Consciousness with a series of questions.

More students than ever seemed to get the concepts and wrote jokes. Every straggler was my personal lost sheep and I would try to work out their brain processes with them. I started to realise that people are infinitely creative but in many different ways. Three joke writing methods weren't enough to incorporate everyone's way of thinking or style of comedy. I needed more and I needed to get away from just word-play. I needed to be able to teach how to be surreal and unusual and come at things from strange and obscure angles.

I was asked if I could double the length of the class for the next year, to 18 hours over six weeks. I said I could.

The six week course was really experimental. It had to be. Half of it was untried. At one stage I made all the students lie on the floor and meander over subjects, which was fun but a tad self-indulgent. I invented The Surrealist Inquisition Question Sheet on the night before one of the classes when I realised I hadn't got enough material to fill it. I now love this method of writing so much that I deeply wish I'd had it when I was a stand-up. But the first time I taught it, I didn't realise that I had to teach the brain process to go with it, and it was a near-disaster. I abandoned it for two years and only resurrected it when, yet again, I was faced with teaching hours to fill and not much to put in them.

I also started experimenting with the stream-of-consciousness way of writing jokes. When I originally tried it with my classes, only one in 10 people got anything out of it. Others did find it cathartic though. I remember one chap writing about his hatred of trains being late, and after 10 minutes of writing non-stop he hadn't got a joke but he was smiling. Having got it out of his system, he felt cleansed and serene. Although I was pleased for him, it was not the effect I was after!

So I tried the directed Stream-of-Consciousness, and gave the class a series of questions and prompts to take up when they ran dry. It stops the repetition and helps really get down to what it is that bothers you. Loads more people wrote jokes that year, which encouraged me to look for more ways to open up the consciousness, which eventually led to the reverse and secret Stream-of-Consciousness which, with the right subject, can be very fruitful.

By that time I'd set up my own dedicated joke writing courses in Hastings on the south east coast of England. The second year, I had the gift of a partially-sighted person in the group. I say gift because up until then apart from the group exercises, I was very focused on getting the students to write. That year I had to spend much longer reading things out loud, repeating things, saying things slowly. I noticed the effect immediately. By doing everything slowly but publicly, the subjects marinated in the room much better and students sparked off the ideas much faster. I know it's a joke *writing* course, but what this student taught me is that, ultimately, jokes are written to be shared, and that the brain responds to the vocalisation faster than it responds to the written word.

So why am I admitting this in a joke writing book? Because I will encourage anyone doing the exercises in this book to say things out loud (yes, even when you're alone – so what if the neighbours think you're mad?) and to share ideas as quickly as possible.

Over the years of teaching joke writing I realised that what I was actually doing was experimenting on the brains of living students, and this has helped me to fine tune what I teach and how I teach it.

I have been in a unique position to develop methods without too much pressure. I've basically had a joke writing lab, and my methods have grown and matured like any fine culture. A few stinky ones have gone off, but on the whole my students have appreciated the experimental nature of the courses, and the result is this book.

I have broken the chapters down into *practical* and *theory* so the reader can dip in and out and take what you want from the book when you need it. One of the comments I've had about the theory chapters is that they are 'different ways of nagging people to get on with it'. I like to think they're inspirational but there's a fine line between being inspired and being nagged! Either way if people end up writing more jokes I'm happy.

I do still write jokes myself and use all my own methods to do so. I was writing jokes for my local MP who was also a Government minister, right up until the 2010 election! This stretched my skills to the limit. Everything had to be politically correct, clean, and taking the mickey out of his policies was an absolute no no. I loved it. Sometimes I wrote a non-PC, slightly risqué joke along the way and sent it to him anyway just to give him a laugh.

A scientist friend of mine told me that when he was a kid he used to pull things apart because he was fascinated by how they worked. That's how I felt about jokes I thought they were the cleverest things in the world. I would roll round the floor in glee when I liked something and spend months just thinking about how just one joke could have been written. Now my friend is a fully fledged scientist and I'm proud to say I have my own joke writing book. I hope you enjoy reading it as much as I have liked writing it.

INTRODUCTION

REDEFINITIONS & PUNS (WARM UP TO WORD-PLAY)

Genius is 99% perspiration, 1% inspiration.
THOMAS A. EDISON

It's a warm October day in Hastings. My new joke writing class sits in a circle. We have just done the introductions.

'Right,' I say, 'I'm going to start with puns.'

A few of them look disappointed.

'Puns are crap, aren't they?' I say.

The disappointed ones look relieved, but a couple of others start to look disappointed. I read them a pun[2]:

My wife's a treasure – people keep asking me where I dug her up.

'Rubbish?' I ask.

The class nod in unison. I read them another one:

Two hydrogen atoms are talking.
One says, 'I think I've lost an electron.'
The other asks, 'Are you sure?'
The first replies, 'Yes, I'm positive.'

---

[2] Unless stated all the puns are from anonymous sources.

This gets a laugh. No-one thinks it's rubbish. We agree that it's still just a pun but it's about a clever subject, so it seems more sophisticated by association.

I am doing this because I want them to see that a joke is a joke is a joke, and we mustn't judge too quickly, because we are about to start writing some. If they won't write down a bad gag, the chances of them writing a good one are very slim.

I read them some more, written by Tim Vine, Britain's foremost pun master:

> *So I said to this gym instructor, 'Can you teach me to do the splits?' He said, 'How flexible are you?' I said, 'I can't make Tuesdays.''*

> *So I said to this train driver, 'I want to go to Paris.' He said, 'Eurostar?' I said, 'I've been on telly but I'm no Dean Martin.'*

> *I was at sea the other day and loads of meat floated past. It was a bit choppy.*

'Good or bad?' I ask.

This is a loaded question now because the class has giggled a bit. Some of them nod, some shake their heads, some are unable to decide and let their heads loll on their shoulders in a confused manner!

I explain to them that the 'choppy' and 'flexible' gags are straight forward puns but the 'Eurostar' joke is slightly different.

Everyone knows that some words, like 'treasure', have two meanings; but take the word 'Eurostar' as in 'You're a star.' It's a new way of thinking about a normal word, so it makes your brain take notice, and seems much more original.

Jokes like the above are what British radio comedy *I'm Sorry I Haven't a Clue* call a Redefinition and the American Washington Post calls Neologism. You take a word or phrase apart, pun on one or both halves of it, and then redefine it. In that way, it doesn't seem as simple as a pun.

These are from *I'm Sorry I Haven't a Clue*, recorded at the London Palladium in 2005:

Randomise... a squint

Kingdom... royal contraceptive

Jugular... a busty vampire

Gondolier... something you catch from a boat man

Mish mash... late for mass due to drunkenness

Urethra... soul singer takes piss

Himalaya... transsexual rooster

Sometimes redefinitions are *so* good that they become jokes in their own right. Try these.

Eric Von Hertz – a German – every time he went through a herd of cows he would shout Ach Dung!
LES DAWSON

Crun: This is Minnie Bannister, the world-famous poker player - give her a good poker and she'll play any tune you like.
SPIKE MILLIGAN

When I was a kid I thought 'racist' meant someone who was good at running. I'd go up to black kids and say, 'You're good at running. I bet when you grow up you are going to be a great racist.'

JASON JOHN WHITEHEAD

I really love language, I used to think bumbling was jewellery for your arse.

TIERNAN DOOYAB

EXERCISE 1: REDEFINING WORDS

Look at these words and see if you can redefine them.

Broadband...

Covenant...

Dialysis...

Endear...

Liability...

Lexicon...

Readiness...

Phonetics...

Hinterland...

Senile...

Answers on the next page...

HOW DID THE CLASS DO?

Broadband...	*fat boy group*
Covenant...	*an insect belonging to witches*
Dialysis...	*phone your sister*
Endear...	*instructions for cockneys about where to stop*
Liability...	*ability to tell fibs*
Lexicon...	*a book of words that aren't real*
Readiness...	*waiting to read a good book*
Phonetics...	*mobile etiquette*
Hinterland...	*place where people never talk about anything directly*
Senile...	*an Egyptian river trip*

Everyone has managed to do some redefinitions and it's interesting how they have interpreted the words differently. There are no right or wrong answers. The same formula can produce different ideas.

One of them has...

Endear – Instructions for cockneys about where to stop

The other has...

Endear – a cockney graveyard

But which do you prefer? I would argue the second version is a more concise redefinition but it has exactly the same meaning as the first – that's where the creativity comes in. Finding the word is the perspiration, redefining it is the inspiration. I send them off for tea and very sweet, chocolaty biscuits (but me? I nibble a carrot dipped in hummus).

EXERCISE 2: FINDING WORDS TO REDEFINE

Once you have got the hang of these, I think the hardest thing is finding words that are redefinable. The first time I taught redefinitions I simply told the class to think of words. You should have seen their faces as they strained to do so. Now I take in the Family Scrabble Dictionary and the Thesaurus (normal dictionaries are no good as they have far too many obscure and unusable words). So now it's your turn.

Look for words to redefine.

If you can't lay your hands on a Thesaurus or Scrabble Dictionary then you can try just looking round your house or through magazines. Or if you want jokes on a particular subject, try thinking of all the things to do with that subject. See if you can find 10 different words to redefine. (If you really have problems, there is some more advice in Troubleshooting at the end of this chapter). Remember not all words are redefinable. The way to tell is to break them down into their syllables and see if they have another meaning.

1...

2...

3...

4...

5...

6...

7...

8...

9...

10...

If you write some good ones, turn them into proper jokes, enter them in the Washington Post Annual Neologies contest, or you can save them for when you're a contestant on *I'm Sorry I Haven't a Clue!*

REDEFINING PHRASES

My class have now all mastered the ability to pull apart any word I give them. It's time to move them on to phrases and sentences. I tell them some more pun-based jokes:

Two fish are in a tank. One says to the other 'Do you know how to drive this thing?'

QUOTED IN – NAKED JAPE BY JIMMY CARR

Why are fish good at wars?
Because they live in tanks.

MY ADAPTATION

They are obviously both the same joke but the first one is clearly better than the second. My class are giving me wry smiles. I read them some more:

> *So I was getting into my car, and this bloke says to me, 'Can you give me a lift?' I said, 'Sure, you look great, the world's your oyster, go for it.'*
>
> **TIM VINE**

> *So I was getting into my car, and this bloke says to me, 'Can you give me a lift?' I said, 'Well I know a bloke who's a lift engineer. He could build one in your house for the right price.'*
>
> **MY ADAPTATION**

The class like the first one better. The difference between them is the difference between wordplay and a simple pun. Tony Allen argues that the pun is a...

> *'meaningless construction that unites two ideas or concepts that have nothing in common other than the fact that they share or have been allocated the same or similar sounding words...word-play or witticism however unites and often adds to the understanding of one or even both words.'*[3]

Take the word 'Draw'. It has a number of meanings: drawing a sketch, drawing a pension, drawing a knife, drawing water, drawing breath, drawing with a pencil, drawing board.

---

[3] Allen, Tony *Attitude - Wanna Make Something of it?* (Gothic Image Publications) 2002 p40

I could write a pun-based joke using that idea:

Reporter: **Do you have problems with teenagers in your art classes?**

Teacher: **Yes they keep drawing knives.**

Here's a word-play based cartoon (based on the same word).

"This is Leonardo Da Vinci drawing his pension - pensions didn't exist in his time but he was a visionary."

It starts out as a pun but gets deeper because it references the fact that Da Vinci envisioned such things as helicopters and was way beyond his time.

But, to write that joke, it had to start out as a pun and then be stretched further. So that's a good reason not to abandon your puns when you first write them. Basically, you can take a simple phrase or saying and interpret it in many different ways. It's a way of thinking that you can learn. The class for this week is nearly over so I set them the next exercise for homework.

EXERCISE 3: NOTICING PUNS & WORDPLAY

Start by looking around you, listening to conversations, watching comedy. Notice how many jokes are based on misunderstanding phrases, and taking words or sayings out of context. Notice puns everywhere. Even the best comics have them. Notice cartoons and headlines in newspapers. Start looking at the words and sentences you write, and see if you can break them up. You will work on these skills in the next few chapters - this is just the beginning. Write down everything that you notice in your note book.

HOW DID THE CLASS DO?

The next week the class brought in headlines from newspapers using puns, and lines from telly programmes (many popular topical shows use puns). One person brought in the book *More Viz Crap Jokes*[4], every single joke in it was the most terrible pun imaginable, but it was somehow compelling to read. One person had written a whole load of fabulous redefinitions and he's kindly let me use them.

Composer...	*a girl modelling on the worldwide web*
Conceit...	*a chair suitable for a villain*
Defile...	*what a Jamaican manicurist uses for de-nails*
Diversion...	*Exit's mission statement*

---

[4] More Viz Crap Jokes. John Brown Publishing Ltd. 1999

Doldrums...	Barbie's percussion instruments
Effluent...	an accomplished blasphemer (this one is very clever)
Expects...	an old pair of glasses
Fundamental...	sponsoring a loony
Ghoulish...	a badly cooked goulash
Gruesome...	home grown vegetables
Inspects...	fashionable glasses
Maritime...	wedding day
Matrimony...	someone who complains in bed
Morass...	big bottomed
Morbid...	a compulsive eBayer (this is my favourite)
Offput...	a bad golf stroke
Outrider...	a gay biker
Potent...	a portable lavvy
Reverse...	poetry recited backwards (this could be a cryptic crossword clue)
Tadpole...	a Polish midget

TROUBLESHOOTING

Problem: I only see double-meanings of words after other people have pointed them out.

Solution: The good news is that you are seeing them. When I get my class to do the redefinitions exercise, I put them into twos and ask them to read to each other from the *Family Scrabble Dictionary* slowly and out loud. I tell them to pause between each word and think about it. If there's no-one to read to then find a quiet room and say them out loud yourself. Spend time with each word. If all else fails, look at the earlier examples and notice how the words break down.

Problem: I feel frustrated reading the dictionary.

Solution: I tell the class only to expect one or two redefinable words per double page spread of the dictionaries, but they *always* want more. Joke writing is often a process, and if you get frustrated, you are saying 'This part of the process is unacceptable'. It's not that difficult to read a dictionary. It might be a bit boring, but if you read it, you will *always* find a couple of words to redefine and you will have probably only been reading for 10 minutes. Why the frustration? I guess it's like sitting in line at a traffic light, hooting your horn. But suppose you thought of it as part of the journey?

Problem: I am writing puns and redefinitions but they are rubbish.

Solution: Puns and redefinitions can be rubbish. They can also be silly, fun and sometimes hilarious. Once your mind gets into word-play, puns (rubbish and otherwise) are a bi-product. If it's a terrible pun, you don't have to tell anyone. Just move on and there might be a good one next time. Word play is just a grown-up pun. If you start the day writing a few puns, by lunchtime you will be on to wordplay, and by the evening you might get a Stream-of-Consciousness gag so deeply funny that by bed-time you rock yourself to sleep laughing.

Problem: I am writing lots of puns but don't know what to do with them.

Solution: If you are a natural punster start by looking at where other people have taken their puns. Spike Milligan used to create wacky characters to give his puns the loveliest of outlets.

Seagoon: Any cases of frozen feet?
Eccles: You didn't order any cases of frozen feet!

Sad Hamlet to Ophelia: 'I'll do a sketch of thee, what kind of pencil shall I use? 2B, or not 2B?'

I turned and rubbed my hands with glee. I always keep a tin of glee handy.

To take your puns to amazing places you can do a joke-web on each half of them (see Chapter 5). Here's one my student did; he didn't just think of one pun and leave it there. He pushed it on and on and on.

My hairdresser never gives me what I ask for. The last time I went I only asked for a trim and they ended up giving me a Mohican. And for a while it was a novelty having my own extinct Native American but it was not what I asked for. But like an idiot I just paid and left. I took him home and cooked him a meal and he refused to eat it. I said, 'I suppose this is the fast of the Mohicans?' But he didn't say anything. About a week later he fell out of a tree and broke his arm. I took him to hospital and, in the car on the way back, I indicated to the white plaster on his arm and said. 'I suppose this is the cast of the Mohicans?' Again he remained silent and impassive, save for a lone tear running down his left cheek. It came to a head one morning when he was filling up his thermos and I grabbed it and said, 'Hey, I suppose this is the flask of the Mohicans?' And he said 'No, no that's not the case and anyway these puns are becoming increasingly laboured as time goes on. Flask doesn't even rhyme with cast. It doesn't scan.' I replied, 'Well I didn't ask for my own extinct Native American in the first place. It was a genuine misunderstanding and it's churlish of you to criticise the material I'm writing for you.' With that he flounced out and I haven't seen him since. There's no punchline but that's often the way with relationships.

When he read his homework to the class he deservedly got a round of applause, it's a fine lesson in pushing your puns to the utmost.

You could also turn your ability to write puns into topical jokes.

Why not take the names of politicians/celebrities and break them up?

Look out for interesting concepts in the news as well. I noticed on telly the other day the comics were having a lovely time reinterpreting the words 'fiscal stimulus'.

Similarly, Phil Jupitus, talking about the Flu Pandemic[5] recently:

'Pandemic? I thought that was flu for Pandas!'

But my favourite is Frankie Boyle's[6] reinterpretation of the so called *Brown Bounce* (the leap in the opinion polls when Gordon Brown took over as Prime Minister) as...

'It sounds like when you put cling film over your toilet bowl!'

SUMMARY

In this chapter we have...

- Learnt how to break up words to create redefinitions and where to look for words to redefine.
- Seen the difference between puns and word-play.
- Watched puns and redefinitions being turned into jokes.

These skills will help you in all your joke writing as you will see in the following chapters.

---

[5] The News Quiz BBC Radio 4 2009
[6] Mock The Week BBC Television 2008

HOW TO USE YOUR BRAIN'S BACKGROUND PROCESSING FUNCTION

To think is to practice brain chemistry.

DEEPAK CHOPRA

I'm always telling my students that if they put in some hard work joke writing, when they go and have a break, their minds will keep working on it, even while they consciously think or talk about something else. How fantastic is that? This is what I call *background processing.*

It really works!

Think about it really hard for a while, then forget about it and it will come to you.

DON DRAPER (MADMEN)

Reece Shearsmith and Steve Pemberton, writers of hit British comedy *League of Gentlemen* say, that despite going to an office every day, their breakthroughs 'very rarely happen when you're actually in the room thinking about it.'

Rather, they happen 'in the middle of the night or while you're at the gym.'[7]

---

[7] speaking on BBC Radio 4, *Front Row* 12/6/09

I've heard it all before. Students often tell me that they put in hours of joke writing to no effect then one came while they were watching telly. Of course it did! But I am certain that without putting in the initial work, without exercising your joke writing muscles, the joke in front of the telly wouldn't have happened.

The brain is amazing. I like to think of it as like one of those early computers, where you put a card in one end, it goes through all sorts of whirring calculations and then the result (in our case, a joke) pops out the other end. The weird thing is that you don't know that your brain has been busy working away, clicking and popping, so it will seem to come from nowhere. That's why you must *always* keep a notebook handy, you never know when it's going to happen.

Before I became a stand-up comic I never wrote a single, what I call a *proper* joke.

> ### Creativity (are you ready for this?) is dreaming while you're awake.
> ROBERT MANKOFF

I was great on the spontaneous, you had to be there type gags but I always wondered who sat down and wrote jokes the moment a news story hit. Not knowing it would eventually be me! The reason that I never wrote a proper joke before I became a stand-up is that I'd never actually set my brain that task, I'd never sat down and tried, I'd never worked on it.

The lesson? You need to show your brain you mean business, get it fully engaged and put in some regular work.

Jerry Seinfeld is said to have had a calendar that he put a big red X on every day that he did his writing tasks. 'After a few days you'll have a chain,' he said. 'Just keep at it and the chain will grow longer every day. You'll like seeing that chain, especially when you get a few weeks under your belt. Your only job is to not break the chain.'[8]

Seinfeld, by setting himself the target of writing every day, is giving his brain lots of time to background process, re-work and re-write. He is not freaking if he doesn't write a joke on a particular day. His aim is just to write.

Every now and then go away, have a little relaxation for when you come back to your work your judgement will be surer.

LEONARDO DA VINCI

The next thing is that he's turning up for the results. I quoted examples above where things just pop into your head but sometimes your head is so full of telly programmes and rock music that it's not until you look at something again that you can see where the joke is. That means re-reading everything. I use a highlighter pen to highlight the merest glimmer of a gag, so by the third re-reading I am just going through the highlighted bits. Often

---

[8] This is from Nudgeblog
http://nudges.wordpress.com/2008/12/12/jerry-seinfelds-commitment-strategy-for-joke-writing/

when I go back to things I see both new ideas and how the old ideas can be used. Obviously my brain's been working away, background processing and is now presenting me with the results.

WHEN YOU'RE UNDER PRESSURE

It's all very well me saying the brain takes its time to come up with things but what if you're on a deadline? You have no time to stop and stare!

Fortunately, your brain doesn't just do background processing while you go for a walk or watch telly. It can work away in the background on one subject or joke idea while you're working on the next. I've done it.

I used to call it wheeling. I'd do as much work as I could on one subject and then when I thought I'd exhausted all ideas, or more precisely couldn't bear to look at it any more, I would move on to the next subject. I'd bang away at that one until I couldn't bear to look that any more either, and then move to the next.

By the time I wheeled round to the first subject again it would look new and interesting, and it would be a relief to look through the ideas I'd already had. Often where I thought I'd run out, my brain would have background processed new ones for me. It's fabulous the way it works.

WHEN YOU HAVE ALL
THE TIME IN THE WORLD

This can be harder because it's so easy to wander off and not do the work when you're not under pressure. How can I, writing this book get you, the person who wants to write jokes, to just sit down and do it?

First of all, answer this. How much time a day can you commit to writing? I think an hour a day is ideal (it doesn't have to be in one block). Half an hour is fine, and I once knew someone with three kids who wrote jokes for 15 minutes a day while they were on the loo. The point is, they made a commitment to doing it at that time and stuck to it.

I always wanted new jokes for my act and if I had no external deadlines I set my own. I would decide I will write for this amount of time, and then do it. I will come back and look at this later, and do it (and often be pleasantly surprised).

My favourite way of working is to do an hour's hard thinking and then go for a walk. Sometimes I consciously set my brain a task, tell it I'd like a good analogy for something, and then a line or a snippet will jump into my head. Trust me, if you really fire up your brain it won't be able to stop working but you have to put the effort in first.

If you are seeking creative ideas go out walking.
Go for a walk. Angels whisper to a man when
he goes for a walk.

RAYMOND INMON

If you're not sure how wonderful this idea is then imagine if garden tools did background processing and, as long as you got hold of your spade and did some serious digging for half an hour, it would carry on digging after you had gone off shopping until it finished the job. Your brain is that powerful. Use it.

SUMMARY

- Background Processing is where you fire your brain up so much by putting loads of thought into a subject that it carries on thinking about it when you take a break or do something else.

- You can prompt this by keep going back to the subject, tickling your brain's neurons, then it will present you with jokes at the oddest of times!

- Always keep a notebook handy so you can catch these thought as they come.

SINGLE JOKE-WEBS

It's Week Two. I'm loaded up with flip chart paper and lots of lovely highlighter pens, which as anyone will tell you are my favourite joke writing tool!

'It's single joke-web week,' I tell the class. 'These joke-webs are single not because they are unloved and can't find a partner but because they're a richly rewarding kingdom in themselves - I was single myself for a long time.' A girl at the back cheers! Thanks, love.

'So far we've looked at puns and redefinitions basically looking outside ourselves for jokes. This is where we open up our minds and learn to free-associate, see where our own thought processes can take a subject. To do this we mustn't be afraid of what we say. We mustn't be afraid of being judged and we mustn't judge others.'[9]

'Ready?' I ask, getting out my flip chart paper. They all nod solemnly and I ask them for a subject.

The class choose STRIKES (as in industrial disputes). I write it down in the middle of a piece of paper and draw a circle round it, and lines coming out of that. I spread the lines wide so I have room to expand. Then I ask the class for associations to do with Strikes. 'Think of big

---

[9] See Chapter 10 for more on this.

things, small things and obscure things,' I say. They come up with the following.

'If this were a mind-map® we would keep free associating outwards, but we want to write jokes so we are going to deliberately forget the original subject of strikes,' I say, clamping my hand firmly down over the word, 'and think about the next level headings in their own right.' I get out my *Ways To Think About Words List* (see next page) to help us along...

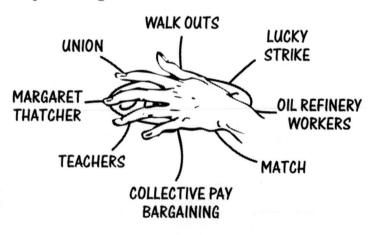

WAYS TO THINK ABOUT WORDS LIST

Break up words and sayings.

Can you replace either of them?

Can you pun on all or half of it?

Take words out of their usual context.

Do the words have another meaning?

See the words historically and socially.

Is there a sound-a-like?

Can you think of an opposite?

Are there any clichés to do with the subject or words?

Add your own here...

'Let's take WALK OUT first (top centre). Forget Strikes just think about Walkouts. See it as two words: WALK and OUT. Can you replace either of them? Take them out of context?'

'Flounce out,' someone says.

'Great,' I say and write it down.

'Do the conga.' Lovely.

'Coming out.' We all laugh.

'Walk on part in a play.' Good.

'Any other way we can say Walk?' I ask.

'Rambling, mincing, power walk,' says the person to my left who's brain is cooking! I write it down.

'Has WALK OUT got an historical context?' I ask.

'Stepping out is an old English term for dating,' someone says.

'Excellent,' I say. 'Is there a good opposite of WALK OUT?' I ask.

'Walk in. Drive in. Crawl out.' It's my free associating friend again. I write them all down.

'So, now we have found new meanings for the words WALK OUT, we can 'remember' our original subject of STRIKES again, and apply them back to create jokes. So take 'FLOUNCE OUT' and think about it in connection with STRIKES.' I say pointing at FLOUNCE OUT on the sheet.

'That might be what the Actor's Union do when they go on strike,' someone says.

'Actually they wouldn't even flounce out they'd exit stage left,' says someone else.

'Wonderful', I say, highlighting FLOUNCE OUT and adding the word ACTORS and STAGE LEFT to it.

Our flow of logic is...

Walk-Out → Flounce Out → Actors → Stage Left

You can see how the joke-web is growing.

'Slightly harder is applying DO THE CONGA to strikes and walk outs,' I say looking round the room hopefully. I needn't have worried as somebody immediately says 'A conga line could be instead of a picket line of a dancers union'.

'Picket line-dancing' says someone else. We all laugh.

'Good, now apply COMING OUT to strikes.'

'Obviously, Gay unionists,' a girl says.

'Obviously,' I reply.

'The Gay Union says, 'Everybody out,' and they say, 'We already are'.' This gets another laugh from the class but I don't stop, I keep pushing them.

'What about applying RAMBLING to strikes and walk outs?' I say.

'A middle class union would go rambling instead of having walk outs,' a student says back. Another great idea. We're on a roll now.

'Good, what about POWER WALKERS and strikes?'

The class now fall over themselves to get to the joke that power walkers walk out and they are 10 miles away before they know it.

There our roll ended. We tried to apply WALK IN back to strikes and got nowhere. Similarly CRAWL yielded nothing except a weak-ish pun about WALKING OUT and CRAWLING BACK IN. I tell the class that not everything can lead to jokes but it's okay because we tried.

'So, now we've got a few ideas, let's see if we can take them to yet another level. So here we have STRIKES -WALKOUT -RAMBLING,' I say, pointing to them on the sheet. That's three levels, let see if we can go down another level. Let's free-associate on RAMBLING. Forget strikes. Forget walk-outs,' I say, clamping my hand down over them on the sheet. 'Just think about rambling.'

'Rambling Rose,' I hear. Good.

'Rambling speech.' Great.

'The Ramblers Association.' Wonderful.

'Rambling would be a male goat's jewellery, Ram Bling!' says a lovely student who hasn't forgotten our redefinitions work of last week. I write them all down.

'Now we remember our original subject of walk outs and strikes,' I say lifting my hand, 'and apply our new meanings to create jokes. Here we go, apply rambling speech and rambling rose etc back to strikes and walkouts.' There's a pause while the students think.

'A union leader could give a rambling speech about a walk-out.' one says eventually.

'If you walk out on a speech that's encouraging you to walk more, is that what the speaker really wants?' says another.

'Do roses join the Ramblers Association?' says a third.

I love it! The students are now so deep into word-play my head's starting to spin and they all look very excited.

'I chose *rambling* first,' I tell them, 'because I could see that it's an easy word to break up and redefine and it has more than one meaning, others might be harder but each time we can follow the same formula.'

The clever bit comes in thinking things through, applying your new meanings back to the main subject and turning them into joke ideas. How far and which paths you go down is up to you. Just follow your intuition. Remember the key is to keep applying the new meaning back to the previous levels.

I set the class the task of finishing the joke-web, which takes the next hour, and the task of doing their own joke-web for homework. I tell them, if they have time, to do a large general joke-web like the one we have just done (Exercise 4).

If not, do a mini joke-web which cuts out the first two levels and goes for specific subjects (Exercise 5).

I also hand out the *Ways To Think About Words List* I was using to prompt their thinking. It should help them to see words in a new light.

EXERCISE 4: SINGLE JOKE-WEBS (GENERAL SUBJECT)

A general joke-web is a major exploration of a subject that you do when you have time, a flask, sandwiches and a torch. Then you can settle down and think of yourself prising open the subject like a clamshell: you are going to explore every nook and cranny, every nuance, and it's going to take at least an hour.

This is going to be a big old joke-web, so get the largest piece of paper you can. I use a flip chart but you can also stick two bits of A4 together.

1. Put your subject in the middle and draw lines coming out. Now think of big things to do with the subject as well as small things and obscure things. Write them all down. These are your sub-subjects.

2. Now clamp your hand down on the original subject and use the *Ways To Think About Words List* to find new meanings and ideas for each of the sub subjects.

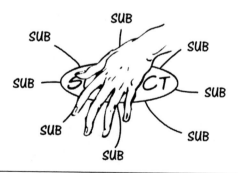

3. Once you have new meanings for your words, apply these back to your original subject, deliberately thinking each one through. Don't dismiss them before you have done this.

4. Go down as many levels as you have space for adding any links you can. This can take you far away from your subject. A completed joke-web should fill every corner of the page. Look at the example joke-web after the *How Did The Class Do?* section in this chapter, and see if yours looks the same.

5. Have a break then read through the whole joke-web, highlighting anything interesting, so when you go back to it again you can just look at what you have highlighted.

6. Then look at everything on the outer rim of the joke-web and apply it back to the central subject. This should throw up strange but interesting juxtapositions.

GENERAL SUBJECT

SUB-SUBJECT
SUB-SUBJECT
SUB-SUBJECT
GENERAL SUBJECT
SUB-SUBJECT
SUB-SUBJECT
SUB-SUBJECT

TO INFINITY...
2nd
2nd
2nd
1st level
SUB-SUBJECT
1st level
2nd
2nd
2nd
2nd
2nd
2nd
2nd
2nd
2nd
2nd
1st level
1st level
1st level
2nd
SUB-SUBJECT
TO INFINITY...
2nd
2nd
2nd
2nd
2nd
1st level
1st level
1st level
2nd
SUB-SUBJECT
1st level
2nd
2nd
2nd
GENERAL SUBJECT
SUB-SUBJECT
1st level
2nd
2nd
1st level
2nd
2nd
2nd
SUB-SUBJECT
1st level
2nd
2nd
2nd
TO INFINITY...
1st level
2nd
2nd
2nd
TO INFINITY...
SUB-SUBJECT
1st level
2nd
2nd
2nd
1st level
2nd
2nd
2nd
TO INFINITY...

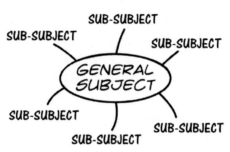

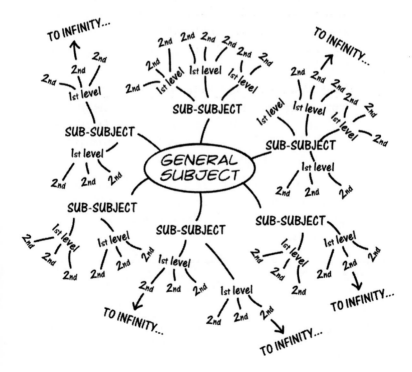

EXERCISE 5: MINI JOKE-WEBS (SPECIFIC SUBJECT)

If you don't have much time you can do a mini joke-web on a specific subject by cutting out the first level of the general joke-web and only going down two levels in total. This can take anywhere from 5 –15 minutes.

1. Find the back of an envelope, shopping list or letter from a utility company that has blank space on it[10].

2. Choose a specific subject. If you find yourself with a general one, break it down, find ONE angle or aspect of it, e.g. don't choose cars, choose seat belts. Don't choose food, choose sub-tropical fruit. Write your subject down on the back of your envelope and draw a circle with lines coming out of it.

3. First of all free-associate on the subject, see it from as many different angles as possible. Top this up by using the *Ways To Think About Words List* to break up any words and phrases. These are your sub-subjects.

4. Put your hand over the initial subject and look at the sub-subjects and free-associate on them, again using *Ways To Think About Words List* if you get stuck.

---

[10] I haven't always recommended using the backs of envelopes but so many students come in with their homework done this way I know it must work!

5. To look for jokes see if you can apply the new meanings of your words back to the original subject. Go through all the associations step by step, like we did in class. Not every association is going to lead to a joke but you must investigate it. Run it through your mind. Check it out. The biggest mistake people make is deciding up front that there are no jokes there (or losing the envelope they wrote them on).

6. Highlight any ideas with a highlighter pen, then when you look at your joke-web again you can just look at the highlighted bits. Also once you have a mini joke-web you can collide it with another joke-web (see Chapter 5) for even more jokes.

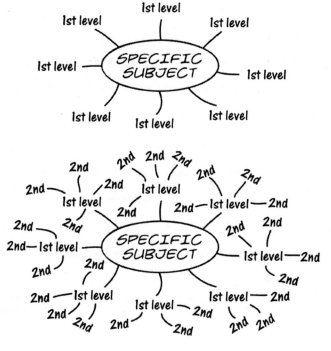

HOW DID THE CLASS DO?

I always get one person who completely loves these and has been up all night with their joke-web, which is so large I have to spread it on the floor. I also get one person who hates them but most people are in the middle and have done pretty well. I have also observed over the years that the amount of jokes students write is nearly always commensurate with the amount of time they put in! Here are some of the jokes they wrote.

We're all getting younger these days. 40 is the new 30. 50 is the new 40. I've even heard that 80 is the new 70.

But don't try that on the motorway!

(Ageing → 80 is new 70 → motorway speeds)

When it snowed recently, they called it a Snow Event. It makes it clear that it doesn't happen very often.

I'm hoping for a Sex Event with my wife soon.

(Snow → Event → Rarely Happens → Sex!)

You get unhinged people – Psychopaths

You get people who can't connect – Sociopaths

And depressed poets - Sylviaplaths

(Psychopaths → Paths → Sylvia Plath)

I poached an egg this morning. The gamekeeper was furious!

(Eggs → Poached → Gamekeeper)

I went on holiday and saw the Wailing Wall and the Bridge of Sighs then I came home to the Underpass of Misery and the Flyover of Indifference.

(Holidays → Wailing Wall → Misery)
(Holidays → Bridge of Sighs → Indifference)

I think it's important we respond to climate change. We do respond in our house, the moment it gets hot we head for the beach. That's a response.

(Respond to Climate change → Hot → Go to the beach)

I don't send money to the third world for water and medicine. They just spend it on drink and drugs.

(Charity → Medicine → Drugs)

I went to a scientist's house it was so posh he had a gene pool in his back garden, however like me, he's Jewish so it was very small.

(Genetics → Gene Pool → Swimming Pool)

Apparently the new national identity card will have penis size on it. I don't mind as long as my identity card is enormous!

(Identity cards → Personal Information → Penis size)

It's the anniversary of the miners strike and I hear the miners and the police have been meeting up on a website called 'Enemies Reunited'.

I used to work for t Ramblers Association used to get a lot o applications... from R

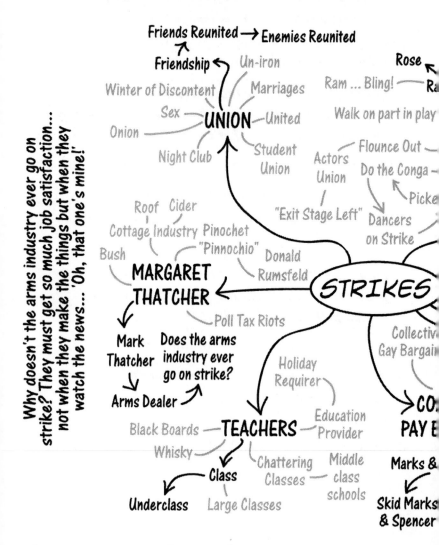

Friends Reunited → Enemies Reunited

Friendship ← Un-iron

Winter of Discontent — Marriages

Sex — **UNION** — United

Onion

Night Club — Student Union

Rose

Ram ... Bling! — Ra

Walk on part in play

Actors Union — Flounce Out

Do the Conga

"Exit Stage Left" — Dancers on Strike

Picke

Roof   Cider

Cottage Industry   Pinochet

Bush — "Pinnochio"

Donald Rumsfeld

MARGARET THATCHER ← **STRIKES**

Poll Tax Riots

Mark Thatcher

Does the arms industry ever go on strike?

Arms Dealer

Holiday Requirer

Collectiv Gay Bargain

CO PAY E

Black Boards — **TEACHERS** — Education Provider

Whisky

Class — Chattering Classes

Middle class schools

Marks &

Underclass   Large Classes

Skid Marks & Spencer

Why doesn't the arms industry ever go on strike? They must get so much job satisfaction... not when they make the things but when they watch the news... 'Oh, that one's mine!

I grew up on a council estate. I went to my local school re-union the other day. We were 'The Underclass of 92'.

Marks and Spencer about the quality o them Skid Mark

It's funny when the whole Olympic squad walks out of the games. With their skills they don't just walk either! Two high-jumped over the wall, three pole-vaulted away and the rest ran a circuit around the back of the stadium.

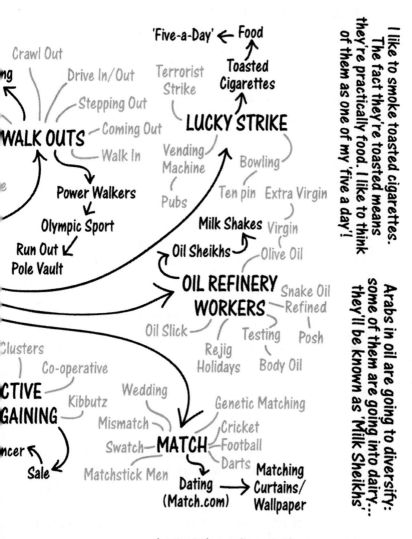

Crawl Out

Drive In/Out

Stepping Out

Coming Out

WALK OUTS

Walk In

Power Walkers

Olympic Sport

Run Out
Pole Vault

'Five-a-Day' ← Food

Terrorist Strike

Toasted Cigarettes

LUCKY STRIKE

Vending Machine

Bowling

Pubs

Ten pin   Extra Virgin

Milk Shakes   Virgin

Oil Sheikhs   Olive Oil

OIL REFINERY
WORKERS   Snake Oil   Refined

Oil Slick   Testing   Posh

Rejig Holidays   Body Oil

Clusters

Co-operative

Wedding

Genetic Matching

CTIVE
GAINING   Kibbutz   Mismatch   Cricket

Swatch—MATCH   Football   Darts

ncer   Sale   Matchstick Men   Dating (Match.com) → Matching Curtains/Wallpaper

I like to smoke toasted cigarettes. The fact they're toasted means they're practically food. I like to think of them as one of my 'five a day'!

Arabs in oil are going to diversify: some of them are going into dairy... they'll be known as 'Milk Sheikhs'

e had complaints
eir pants. I call
nd Spencer!

I tried the online dating agency - Match.com and found out that I'm perfectly matched with some 1970's wallpaper

TROUBLESHOOTING

Problem: I did a joke-web and got no jokes.

Solution: Joke-webs with no jokes on them tend to be sad neglected specimens with only a few associations and nothing followed through. I know some people find it hard to think of things to put on their joke-webs, which is why I have included the *Ways To Think about Words List*. Some people do great joke-webs just by free-associating, but the list makes sure you are covering every angle. Take a look at these two subsections of real joke-webs, both done on the same subject.

This joke-web just lists makes of cars. They are meaningless words, so the only way they could yield ideas is if you could pun on them. Also, listing them rather than spreading them doesn't give any space for more associations.

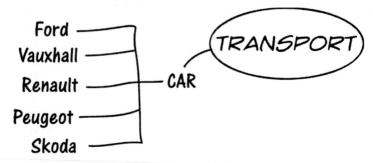

Now look at the word CAR, temporarily forgetting the original subject (which was transport). This joke-web has cable car and toy car, school run - something you need a car for, Jimmy Carr - a pun on car, cartoon - a half pun, and horseless carriage - thinking about car in its historical context.

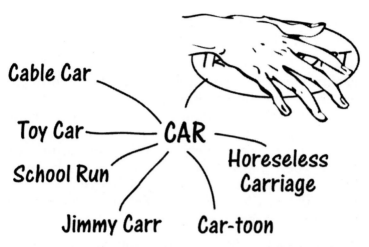

Cable Car

Toy Car — CAR

School Run

Horeseless Carriage

Jimmy Carr   Car-toon

Now we have done this, we can *remember* our original subject and apply our new car meanings back to transport problems. I don't think getting rid of Jimmy Carr will solve our transport problems.

Then try applying 'toy car' back to the original concept of traffic problems. Do kids with toy cars get traffic jams in their rooms? That's a nice idea.

Then go down another level and start thinking of other things to do with traffic jams and see if they apply to kids playing with toy cars.

My kid has got so many cars that his bedroom looks like the M25 during rush hour.

He's six. He's already got road rage.

Mind you I did dock his pocket money to pay the congestion charge.

As you can see, this is a much more fruitful way of using joke-webs.

Question: Why do I find it hard to make joke-webs work when I'm on my own?

Answer: That might be because when you do a group joke-web, you talk each stage through, which makes you think each stage through. If you do a joke-web on your own and just glance at the result you could miss loads of jokes. The answer is to be a crazy joke writer, say things out loud even if you are on your own and the joy is, because you're on your own no-one is judging you. You can follow the craziest of ideas. Let the joke-web be your friend and muse.

If that doesn't work I suggest you find yourself a writing partner!

Problem: I feel like I don't want to write anything down on my joke-web unless I'm sure it's going to lead to a good joke.

Solution: First of all, congratulations for identifying the problem. So many people feel like this. There are lots of reasons why people won't write things down (or say things out loud when in a group situation, see Chapter 10 for more on this). I remember teaching one class when we were doing a joke-web on bird flu which had just broken out on Bernard Matthew's farm. We had gone down several levels and were coming up with nothing. Eventually I had to ask 'Are any of you holding anything back? We can say anything here. It doesn't matter if it's rude.' (I thought that might be the problem).

One bloke winced. 'Well,' he said, 'I am, not because it's rude but because it's too boring.'

'What is it?' I asked.

'Well bird-flu is the H5 N1 virus,' he said meekly.

'Great,' I said and wrote it down.

The moment we disassociated it from the original subject of Bird Flu it was clear that H5 N1 looks like either a postcode or car number plate. Within a minute the class had written a gag about Bernard Matthews' postcode being H5 N1 and we all gave a sigh of relief. The lesson there is that you have to suspend disbelief, write everything down, don't prejudge, and follow every lead.

Question: Do you believe that joke-webs always work if you do them right?

Answer: Clever question. I can honestly say that in a classroom situation I have always managed to find some jokes on whatever subject the class set, and usually it's an impressive crop of gags. But there again in class I do a big general joke-web, I have at least eight brains thinking and can give it up to an hour. When I do mini joke-webs at home alone, every now and then I've had one where I've only got a few weak puns out of it.

If I'm stuck I always double check the *Ways To Think About Words List* because it's usually my thinking that's stuck. I also start doing and thinking deliberately as if there was a class there, applying things back to the previous subject.

Generally I know that if I have thought really hard about words, sayings and phrases on my joke-web, thought of alternative meanings and contexts for them all, even tried to look for a sound-alike, had a break from it and then gone back through all of the associations, then I can be more than happy in the knowledge that I have explored that association, and move on to the next one. I usually do two mini joke-webs at a time so it's not so upsetting if one doesn't work out.

Question: What's the difference between general and mini joke-webs?

Answer: A general joke-web is a collection of smaller joke-webs all grouped around a large general subject that goes down many levels stretching far and beyond the original subject. A mini joke-web targets a specific subject and just goes down two levels.

SUMMARY

- Joke-webs are a wonderful tool for opening up a subject and finding all its nuances and angles.

- The key to all joke-webs is, once you are past the first layer, to forget the original subject to create new meaning for words and phrases and then apply them back to create jokes.

- The more you put into a joke-web the more you will get out.

JOKES EXIST IN THE ETHER!

*Where the ideas come from I don't know...
it was inspiration, but I know not from where.*

SPIKE MILLIGAN

You've got your dream job. Brilliant! You're a writer on a topical comedy show when a big, huge, you can't avoid it news story breaks. Say a politician has resigned. You think it's a shame as you were hoping to lead on a celebrity boob job story. However you can't tell your team there are no jokes on the politician resigning. They wouldn't believe you anyway. Within minutes of any news story breaking jokes start flying round the internet. You can't nick jokes from the internet though. Your jokes have to be original and acceptable to a mainstream audience.

But in reality this wouldn't happen. If you really were a writer on a topical show you'd already know that no matter what the story, you can find jokes on it and you would have ways of tracking them down.

In Chapters One and Three you saw that it's not genius to realise that something can have a double meaning but it is clever to link words that haven't been linked before to make a new joke from them.

I think those links exist already: they are Jokes in the Ether. Others have called it other things. It's not a new concept. But to those who don't know, it does sound a bit kooky, as if you need to go to a séance to get new jokes. Let's try it.

"Are there any jokes out there?
Knock once for yes, twice for no..."

"Oh no, I don't want 'Knock Knock' jokes!"

This cartoon is literally a joke in the ether because it takes two normally unconnected subjects (séances and joke writing), and finds a link (knock knock) and turns it into a joke. That link existed before we came along – it was there waiting to be found.

(P)eople say they write songs, but in a way you're more the medium. I feel like all the songs in the world are just floating around, it's just a matter of like an antenna, of whatever you pick up

KEITH RICHARD

Even surreal jokes are based on unusual angles or twists on subjects - you just have to find them. You don't need sinewy brain power, you just have to know how and where to look, and keep at it. In 1998 I did a writing audition for a TV company making the *11 O'clock Show* for Channel 4. I was given the task of writing as many jokes as possible over three days, but only on subjects that were in the newspapers on those days.

This was mid-August.

It was hot, everyone exciting was abroad, and nothing much was happening in the world. I discussed it with a fellow comic who was doing the same audition. He agreed –there was nothing in the news. I spoke to friends about it who also told me there was nothing in the news. But there was. Newspapers were still being printed every day. They still had the same number of pages. Topical radio and telly programmes were still going ahead. They would have to work with what was there. I decided to do the same.

If you do not seek you will not find.

SOPHOCLES

I flicked a paper open. There was a story about purpose-built offices for politicians being built next to the House of Commons, another one about new trading standards rules, and then, hidden away in the corner, a couple of lines about Prince William taking driving lessons. For the next three days I pored over every line of every newspaper, over and over again. I hunted in the subtext, in the picture headings, in the last line of the longest paragraph, and I knew that, no matter how dull the story, I could find links, angles and juxtapositions to make it more interesting[11].

I did joke-webs.

I broke words apart and put them back together in new ways.

Eventually I wrote jokes about special alterations being made to the building for politicians to make it easier for them to sleep with their secretaries. I then applied the new trading standards rules to things they normally don't regulate, such as bra sizes, and wrote a visual joke (it was for telly after all) about Prince William driving as part of a royal cavalcade, with all 30 cars reversing at once. I got the job.

My friend didn't send anything in. When I saw him, he mimed flicking through the newspapers.

'There was nothing in them,' he said.

The truth he hadn't looked properly in the papers or in the ether. He thought that a good joke comes from a good news story.

---

[11] Chapter 7 deals with this method of writing topical jokes in detail.

This experience taught me that there exists somewhere, a joke on every subject in the world, even dull news stories. You just have to put the effort in to find it.

It seems to me that most of the jokes I make already exist Out There in some strange realm of ideas, and that the comedian travels towards them.

LOGAN MURRAY

Also, once you really understand that jokes exist in the ether, you can stop beating yourself up when you find corny jokes, rude jokes or rubbish jokes. You just found those jokes there. You don't have to use them.

In fact when I start writing on any subject I get the puns out of the way first. Puns exist, words have double meanings, and they are bound to be my first port of call on the search for jokes. Sometimes I can use them as a basis for a better joke. Sometimes I tell them to a friend just to hear them groan.

Which brings me to my final point.

Just trusting jokes are there and not putting any effort in, doesn't work I'm afraid.

Pray to catch the bus but run like hell for it anyway.

ANON

I've tried it. You've tried it. You have to put the time in. Believe me at my joke writing courses I don't just teach them that jokes exist in the ether and tell them to sit and wait for them to turn up. Oh, how great that would be! We get busy with the exercises, crank up our brains and *then* they really do appear...

SUMMARY

- You don't have to be a genius to write jokes, they exist in the ether!

- You just need to spend time looking for them! Why not start now?

DOUBLE JOKE–WEBS & THE HADRON JOKE COLLIDER

The Large Hadron Collider will accelerate bunches of protons... colliding them head-on..., with each collision spewing out thousands of particles at nearly the speed of light.

SCIENTIFIC AMERICAN

The Hadron Joke Collider will bash two opposing subjects together, colliding them head-on with the collision spewing out jokes at the speed of thought.

ME

It's Week Three of the class and I get them playing some improv games as a bit of a warm up[12]. They've enjoyed romping round the room but it's time for something more cerebral. I sit them down and ask them if they've heard of the Large Hadron Collider. Most of them have, although they've no idea why I'm mentioning it.

'We're going to use a similar concept to write jokes,' I tell them. Loads of jokes are links between two previously unrelated subjects. I tell them a joke...

---

[12] See Logan Murray's book Be *How to be a Great Stand-up* (Hodder) 2010 for more about great improv games to play.

*I love it that politicians are coming out as bisexual.
On election night the swingometer will at last be able
to swing both ways!*

'That joke was written by doing two joke-webs, one on politicians and one on sexuality,' I say, showing them two joke-webs.

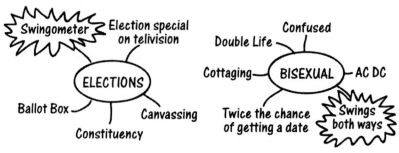

'The writer (okay, me) spotted the link between SWINGOMETER and SWINGS BOTH WAYS. That link already existed between the two subjects. It was there waiting for me to find it.'

I then get all mystical and explain my theory of Jokes in the Ether (see previous chapter).

'However, it's not always that straightforward. Other links are more subtle and have to be pushed. That's where the *Hadron Joke Collider* comes in,' I say, smiling, because I love this concept.

'I'll show you,' I say. 'First of all we need two subjects to bash together.'

The class choose ART and RELATIONSHIPS even though some of them don't know anything about art and others know even less about relationships!

I get out my enormous flip chart (I always want plenty of room for their ideas) and start the first joke-web. I ask for associations to do with RELATIONSHIPS. The class comes up with the following.

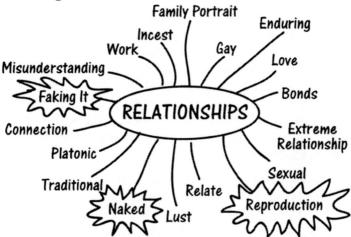

Then I do the same with Art... I have highlighted the obvious links between the subjects that came up immediately.

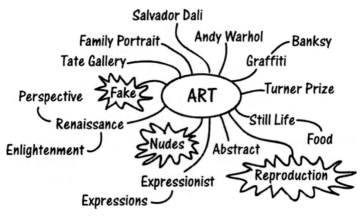

This class are very clever and full of ideas so this stage takes us about 20 minutes. I only ask them for one layer of associations but sometimes they free associate down, as with Renaissance, so I write it down (I always go with the flow).

The class are sitting back in their seats, they think the work is done, but the most creative stage is just starting - the one where we collide the subjects into each other. I tell them we are going to apply everything from the RELATIONSHIPS joke-web to the central subject of ART and have a think about it, no matter how ridiculous the initial idea seems, and then do the same with Art and Relationships.

A few words already appear on ART and RELATIONSHIPS such as naked/nudes, faking it /fake and reproduction. I know we might be able to turn these into ideas, but we want more than that – don't we?

We start with ANDY WARHOL and apply him and his ideas to RELATIONSHIPS.

We think in silence for quite a while before someone comes up with the idea of having *pop relationships* instead of *pop art*. Then we re-apply his famous quote about everyone being famous for 15 minutes to everyone being in a relationship for 15 minutes, which naturally leads to the idea that for some people that would be too long! A good start.

We carrying on working for the next 40 minutes, crashing ideas from one of the joke-webs against the main subject of the other. Here are the ideas we came up with. As usual, some are good, some are weak but they are all great work-out for our joke writing muscles. We got another five jokes and a few more ideas that I have explained in 'Glimmers of gags' below. Even if you only went on to sell or use one of them I would say that was worth it.

'I come from a very dysfunctional family, we had to have our family portrait done by Salvador Dali.' [13]

(FAMILY applied to ART)

'I went out with an art dealer once. It didn't work out because he could tell my orgasms were fake.'

(FAKING IT was on both joke-webs, the creativity was how to use it)

I had a friend who was an expressionist painter. She was going great until she started having botox!

(Expressionist Paintings → Facial Expressions → Botox) [14]

I went to Tate & Lyle's head office. They love sugar so much even their art was cubist.

(Tate Gallery → Tate & Lyle → Sugar → Cube → Cubist)

My boyfriend was worried about me moving in so I explained to him that I'm an artist like Tracey Emin and I'm using his flat as a gallery to display my

---

[13] We liked the ideas that different types of art could represent different types of family relationships and bashed around several ideas before this one stuck.

[14] This was a double joke-web working like a single one, which of course happens and is a lovely bonus.

installation. This one is called 'dirty knickers on the floor'.

(INSTALLATION applied to relationships)

'I tried art classes but I can't do a still life of any food because I'd eat it before I'd finished the painting.[15]

(STILL LIFE applied to the student's relationship with food)

GLIMMERS OF GAGS

We study *all* the others but draw some blanks which is fine, as long as we try. Sometimes we see what I call 'glimmers of gags', where you catch the chance of a gag, a wisp of a funny.

We try very hard with REPRODUCTION, which appears in both sides and covers everything from a womb to a photocopier. Could a girl be going out with a doctor, a specialist in reproduction only to find out she's dating the photocopier guy? One person also used the nude/naked juxtaposition to come up with 'I love art, you get to see naked people without going out with them' but we felt it had been done before.

We also have a go at bashing the word RENAISSANCE against relationships. We talk about how in the Renaissance they found perspective. We wonder if during the actual Renaissance many marriages changed as people started to get their

---

[15] One of the students came out with this joke fully formed, when we looked at Still Life. This student does a lot of jokes about eating. This would fit in perfectly with her act, I tell her to write it down and use it.

relationships in perspective (I think this is a lovely idea - we just couldn't get it into a gag).

The more interesting ideas have definitely come from the deliberate bashing of one subject against another, that wouldn't normally be juxtaposed. I set the class homework of doing more joke-webs and we talk about how to choose topics (see below). I also hand out the *Ways To Think About Words List* (again - most of them have already lost the one I gave out last week!)

WAYS TO THINK ABOUT WORDS LIST

Break up words and sayings.

Can you replace either of them?

Can you pun on all or half of it?

Take words out of their usual context.

Do the words have another meaning?

See the words historically and socially.

Is there a sound-a-like?

Can you think of an opposite?

Are there any clichés to do with the subject or words?

HOW TO CHOOSE A TOPIC

Try two random ideas as we did earlier.

Sometimes stories in the news are ripe for double joke-webs; look for politicians with weird hobbies (do one joke-web on politics, one on the hobby), celebrity stories, offbeat news items like police storing DNA with ice-cream (do one joke-web on DNA, one joke-web on ice-cream). Look for scientific ideas such as monkeys in space (do one joke-web on monkeys, one joke-web on space) etc.

If you find a good pun, do a joke-web on each half of it, e.g. you might take the example of reproduction that we found above and do two joke-webs one on photocopiers, one on wombs.

Try and find contradictions in your own life, e.g. wanting a new partner but can't be bothered to dress up and go out and look for one.

Break up popular sayings such as General Hospital (do one joke-web on General and one on Hospital) and Surfing the Net (one on Surfing, one on Nets).

The world is changing and to cope with it we are inventing new words all the time. Think of these words as NPOs (New Pun Opportunities!) Be the first to pun on them. Examples are bi-polar (we just used to be manically depressed) and IVF cycle (you had to adopt). Both of those have been used in this book but by the time this is in the shops there will be more.

If you're a stand-up, story teller or monologist see if you can find links between the subjects you already talk about. This will help the flow of your set.

Have you found a subject? Then you are ready to do the next exercise.

EXERCISE 6: DOUBLE JOKE-WEB

Get an A4 piece of paper, or two smaller ones, one for each joke-web

Choose two subjects.

Write for at least 10 minutes on each joke-web. Write everything down that comes into your head. Think of the big things that go with a subject, the small things, the people, the locations, the concepts and the history associated with it. If you're stuck use the *Ways To Think About Words List.*

Put it in your Hadron Joke Collider. Apply *every* concept from one joke-web to the MAIN SUBJECT of the other joke-web.

Think it through for a few seconds, no matter how crazy it seems. Write ALL ideas down no matter how weak they feel.

Look at your list of ideas and see which you can turn into gags. Keep going back, keep reconsidering, keep thinking.

Remember! You are an intrepid joke explorer. The more you explore the more jokes you will find.

HOW DID THE CLASS DO?

Here's some of the jokes the class wrote. It fascinates me the subjects that people choose and the creativity that erupts when you start to collide them. It's a great way of staying original and finding new things to joke about - it's as innovative as the Hadron Joke Collider itself!

This was a joke-web on animal bonding collided against a joke-web on relationships...

He had the sex drive of an animal - unfortunately it was a panda.

Though that did mean he was very attractive - unfortunately to flies.

This was a joke-web on women collided against a joke-web on the third world...

Do you get anorexics in Africa? When the famine comes along they must go 'Yes, Result!'

This was a joke-web on camping collided against a joke-web on the Greek Island of Lesbos...

I went on holiday to Lesbos and came back covered in bites - Those lesbians are naughty!

This was a joke-web on accountancy collided with one on gardening...

I'm an accountant and a gardener, people say isn't that boring? They've obviously never seen a square root.

This was a joke-web on bi-polar disorder collided against a joke-web on relationships...

> *I was a manic depressive. Men didn't have relationships with me they just went on bi-polar expeditions. I'm very easy to break up with they just say, I'm going out now, I may be some time.*

This was a joke-web the economy collided against a joke-web on hospitals...

> *The British economy was rushed to hospital today. But it's okay it's just broken its Footsie.*[16]

TROUBLESHOOTING

Problem: I did a couple of joke-webs but didn't get any ideas.

Solution: Really? Not a single one? Well, firstly, are you using the *Ways To Think About Words List*? It's really helpful for finding associations. Then, the most crucial stage is to apply every association from one side of the joke-web to the *main subject* of other subject, and vice versa, and think about each one. Not just glance at it, but really think about it.

The Hadron Collider bashes atoms together at great speed and intensity with spectacular results. This can happen with colliding joke-webs, but basically the Hadron Joke Collider *is your brain* and you need to think really hard. Why not lie on the floor and think about it? Go for a walk and

---

[16] For overseas readers the FTSE (pronounced Footsie) is the Financial Times Stock Exchange Index.

keep thinking about it. Bash those subjects together. Whizz them round your brain. If nothing else, this is a great brain work-out.

Problem: If I don't get a joke straight away I find myself giving up.

Solution: Lots of people feel like this. For an experienced joke writer who spends at least an hour a day writing, it doesn't matter so much if you spend 10 minutes bashing one subject against another and there isn't a joke there. But for a new joke writer, it's heart-breaking. I included the ideas that didn't work when I wrote up the class example to illustrate that they don't all work out and that it's important to keep going. Try and think of yourself as an intrepid joke-prospector: we know there's joke gold there in that river, and we've got to sieve through some earth to find it. Each time you bash an association against the other subject, that's a little shake of your sieve, and, if you keep sieving, there will be gold in your pan.

Problem: I've done two joke-webs and there aren't any links common to both.

Solution: I know in the class example there were three direct links but most of the jokes came from the next stage of the exercise such as applying 'Art Installation' to 'Relationships' and doing the big thinking. When you first do a double joke-web and find links it's a lovely bonus and it does happen a lot. But it would be a shame if that's all you did a double joke-web for, when there's so much more to find. The other thing is that the obvious links can lead to obvious jokes. When you collide subjects you will find the deeper less obvious ideas which lead to profound jokes, thoughts and musings - a truly wonderful thing.

Don't forget...

> *The purpose of the Large Hadron Collider is to increase our knowledge about the universe.*
> HOW STUFF WORKS

> *The purpose of the Hadron Joke Collider is to increase the number of jokes in the world.*
> ME

SUMMARY

- Many jokes are links between two subjects.

- You can push these links further by using the Hadron Joke Collider to bash subjects together.

- The real key to it is to think each one through no matter how crazy or unconnected it seems.

PANIC IS THE ENEMY OF JOKE WRITING

We cannot escape fear. We can only transform it into a companion that accompanies us on all our exciting adventures.

SUSAN JEFFERS

The best and most creative of people panic. I recently watched an old film of Paul McCartney singing *Yesterday* at the Royal Variety Performance[17]. He'd never sung it in public before and you can clearly see the beads of sweat on his forehead. The caption underneath said that Paul McCartney admitted later he was really nervous because he thought the song was no good and everyone would hate it!

The good thing is he still went out and sang it.

So if you accept that we all panic, the only difference between a creative person who does things, and someone paralysed into displacement activity, is that the doers have learnt to put their panic to one side, keep doing the work and trusting their process.

I think there are three broad types of joke writers' panic:

---

[17] TOTP2 Captions by Steve Wright (BBC2)

1. I'LL NEVER BE ABLE TO WRITE JOKES ON THIS SUBJECT!

This kind of panic stops you starting and often leads to displacement activity - all those cups of tea and a sudden need to clean the bathroom. If you do manage to start working, this kind of panic can mean that if you don't write jokes in the first three minutes you give up.

2. IT HAS TO BE PERFECT!

This kind of panic means that even if you do start work and you find some joke ideas, you will decide none of them are good enough, none of them are worth following up, and you will abandon them like babies in a basket without honing them or going back to them, making all the work you put in a complete waste of time.

3. EVERYONE WILL THINK THIS IS RUBBISH!

Even if you have ideas you thought were okay, when it comes to sharing them you suddenly lose faith. Your mouth will be too dry to say them aloud and your heart will be fluttery. The jokes never see the light of day. Then one day you will find a screwed up bit of paper in the bottom of the wardrobe, read them again and realise that some of them were funny after all but sadly now long out of date.

I'm sure we all have our own weird and very special variations of panic. But any form of panic sucks away your brain power, your energy, and your will. Suppressing it can just make it worse.

My way of dealing with it is to accept that it's there.

I say 'Yup, these are my nerves, I always have them,' and then I keep on working, keep sifting through ideas, keep looking for new angles, and try to see doing the work and putting in the time as my goal.

> *The trick with dealing with fear is to*
> *go on in spite of feeling afraid.*
> **JUDY CARTER**

I know that when I'm working I don't have 100% guarantee that I am going to write a brilliant joke, but if I allow my panic to stop me working, I'm 100% guaranteed I won't write anything.

If you still want to focus on all that is wrong, then psychiatrist Robert Leahy[18] recommends *worry postponement* where you schedule time to fret about things later, and, according to essayist Anne Lamont,[19] you can suspend perfectionism as well by putting off any brain activity that stops you getting on with your work, and telling yourself you can worry, panic and/or make it perfect later.

If you need some outside influence to help you focus, then invite joke writing friends round to do an exercise together. Allow yourself to write anything as long as you are writing.

The panic won't go away completely. Every time I start writing jokes I worry that this is the time there will be none, this time I will fail. I counter it by telling myself that even if that is so then I will

---

[18] Robert Leahy, *Anxiety Free. Unravel your fears before they unravel you.* Published by Hay House
[19] *Bird by Bird* by Anne Lamont

still do my best, and run whatever subject through my joke writing methods, and put the time in.

I have learnt to live with my fears.

So take a deep breath. Feel those nerves. They're kind of exciting aren't they? After all, it's a special thing to be allowing yourself time to write jokes. Let the nerves sit there in your stomach or spleen (or bowel if you are really unlucky) while you get on with the exercise. Write out those associations. Do the work. Find those angles. Don't focus on the panic, use it! Let the adrenalin help your brain think faster.

Boldness has genius, magic and power in it.
Begin it, begin it now.
GOETHE

We're all the same, you know. You, me, the writers of great sitcoms, famous stand-up comedians. We all panic because we're doing something exciting that isn't working at a factory or sitting in the pub. We are joke writers and thinkers, and it's scary, but oh so rewarding.

SUMMARY

- Panic is natural – accept that
- Don't engage with it - walk beside it
- Just keep working

WRITING JOKES FROM NEWSPAPERS

The crisis of today is the joke of tomorrow.

H. G. WELLS

'Suppose I told you that a lot of topical jokes you hear on the radio or telly aren't really topical jokes,' I say to my class. It's Week Four of the course and they are all sitting with the newspapers I asked them to bring in. They look up at me, not sure what to say.

'A lot of topical jokes are normal jokes masquerading as topical jokes' I assert. 'Let me prove it...'

I tell them a joke from the Chair's script on *Have I Got News for You*, written about the Queen's tour of Italy. It takes a quote from a newspaper:

The Queen spent a long time staring at the ceiling of the Sistine Chapel

The punchline is:

She hasn't done that since her wedding night.

I argue that this is not actually a topical joke about the Queen touring Italy. It makes no comment about the Royal family, and has nothing to say about Rome, our foreign policy or the tour itself. It's a simple play on the words staring at the ceiling.

But as long as some joke is made and the set-up comes from a current newspaper, the audience laugh, the presenter smiles and no-one's the wiser.

My class look intrigued.

'I'm not knocking it, by the way,' I say. 'This is a fabulous way to write topical jokes for your acts, cartoons or sketches. I go on to tell them a joke from Radio 4's *The News Quiz*, delivered by the Chair, Sandy Toksvig:

> *The Government are stopping people who foster extremist views from coming into the country.*
>
> *I tried to foster an extremist view once, but social services said my house wasn't big enough.*[20]

That joke doesn't comment on the state of racism in the country or that the Government had denied a Dutch fascist entry. It's simply a pun on the word foster – another example of a non-topical joke happily masquerading as a topical joke, on a topical news show.

To write jokes like this, you have to focus on the wording of a story, and this is where the newspapers come in. Instead of writing jokes about the news story in general, you simply look for interesting lines that you can play off. So, for example, when there were fires in California, *Have I Got News for You* put this newspaper quote on the screen:

> *They had to douse fire with whatever they could get their hands on.*

---

[20] The News Quiz 9th May 09

It's a great sentence to pick out because it opens up all the stereotypes about Californians. I ask my students what kind of things Californians might be able to get their hands on.

'Gallons of anti-wrinkle cream' says one.

'Wheatgrass juice' says another.

'Fake breasts' says one of my more surreal students and we all get an image of silicone implants being hurled at a fire. The actual joke was:

They had to douse fire with whatever they could get their hands on - organic jojoba, carrot juice and, in one case, water.

Which is no better or worse than what the class came out with. It doesn't matter which stereotypes about Californians you use. This method of writing jokes means you can avoid tackling the tragic story of the fires head-on and foist a non-topical idea onto a topical subject.

Stereotypes are great in this method of joke writing. When George W. Bush had his watch stolen, a number of topical shows took the angle of what his watch might be like, or whether he could tell the time, again avoiding the actual subject of the watch being stolen. Other stereotypes used by satirical shows are that the lovely David Beckham is a bit thick, while Jordan, Posh, Paris Hilton, etc, are seen as shallow bimbos. Ex-President Clinton is usually portrayed as randy, Boris Johnson as a buffoon, Prince Philip is a racist and all British MPs are now seen as on the fiddle. Topical gag writers use stereotypes as short-hand in jokes and so can you.

EXERCISE 7: WRITING PUNCHLINES FROM SET-UPS

Look at the following set-up lines from satirical news shows over the years and see if you can find the joke. For people doing this home alone, give yourself about half an hour, maybe in two 15-minute bursts. I'm giving my class 20 minutes because I have put them into groups of four, so it's easier for them.

SAUDI ARABIAN MINISTER VISITS BRITAIN

Set up: The Queen rolled out the red carpet

Punchline ....

....

....

HUGH FEARNLEY-WHITTINGSTALL

(Who was in the studio when this joke was done.)

Set up: One female journalist visited Hugh Fearnley-Whittingstall and felt sick when he presented her with an entire tongue, curled round fatly in the shape of a question mark

Punchline ....

....

....

DAVID BECKHAM HAS HAD CORN ROWS PLATTED INTO HIS HAIR

Set up: After his visit to the hairdresser he said that his head 'hurt for a while'

Punchline ....

....

....

TONY BLAIR

(This was from a story about rising oil prices.)

Set up: Mr Blair should remember how many people have car keys...

Punchline ....

....

....

HOW DID THE CLASS DO?

When I do this exercise I'm fascinated by the sheer range of jokes that I get back from just offering my class a few sentences. I'm actually convinced that I could give a group any sentence and tell them there is a joke there and they would come up with something, because they *trust* that a joke is there. Also, how often do you spend time staring at one sentence, looking at every connotation? As I usually put people in groups of four so there's all that brain power going over just a few words. It's not surprising that for the one sentence I get three or four jokes back.

Here's what I got back from my class, and underneath is the joke that was originally broadcast. The point of the exercise is *not* to get it 'right,' it's just to get you into that way of thinking, and show you how professional programmes work.

SAUDI ARABIAN MINISTER VISITS BRITAIN

The Queen rolled out the red carpet...

Class Answers:[21]

...but he decided to buy a Persian rug instead.

...Prince Philip rolled out after.

...though next time she's going for wood flooring.

...whilst round the back Prince Harry rolled up a spliff.

Broadcast punchline:

The Saudi Arabian minister said I could have got that for you half price.

---

[21] This is interesting because from six words 'the Queen rolled out the red carpet,' we've got four different jokes. 1) plays off the stereotype of Arabs, 2) takes the sentence literally that the Queen rolled out of the red carpet, 3) gives an alternative for carpet 4) looks at other things you can roll. Not a bad haul.

HUGH FEARNLEY-WHITTINGSTALL

One female journalist visited Hugh Fearnley-Whittingstall and felt sick when he presented her with an 'entire tongue, curled round fatly in the shape of a question mark'

Class Answers:[22]

...Not as sick as when he invited her to taste his semi-colon.

...Imagine where the exclamation mark came from.

...She had to be carted away in an ambulance when he showed her his penis.

...She was already full up with his Cumberland sausage.

...But he knew the answer would be a smack in the chops.

Broadcast punchline:

He admitted it was a bit much for a first date.

---

[22] 1) and 2) work on the fact that it is a question mark with 5) adding in its own double play on the word chops. 3) and 4) work on the notion that the journalist felt sick and take it a step further.

DAVID BECKHAM HAS HAD CORN ROWS PLATTED INTO HIS HAIR

He said after his visit to the hairdresser that his head 'hurt for a while'...

Class Answers:[23]

...All she'd asked was whether he was going anywhere for his holiday.

...It was the liveliest activity close to his brain for a long time.

...Next time he won't try and read Heat magazine.

...after taking his head out of the boiling pan but the corn was cooked to perfection.

...Victoria suggested he use a comb not a combine harvester.

...He should be used to suffering being married to Posh.

Broadcast punchline:

That was just working out 10% of the bill for the tip.

---

[23] This set-up always gets the biggest haul of gags. 1), 2), 3) play off the David Beckham is thick stereotype. 4) and 5) are a quite clever play off corn rows whilst 6) goes for the jugular with Victoria Beckham.

TONY BLAIR

Mr Blair should remember how many people have car keys...

Class Answers:[24]

He picked enough out of bowls in his time.

...and tax the bastards.

No cars – just keys.

He couldn't check because the Government lost the data again.

Broadcast punchline:

...and not one of them would be pleased to get Cherie at a wife swapping party.

---

[24] 1) is playing off the word Keys, which is the angle the show went on as well. 2) is very original and probably better than the joke the show used, 3) is a lovely pun really, that takes the sentence literally and 4) alludes to another topical story that was in the news at the time about the Government losing data.

FINDING YOUR OWN SET-UPS

My class are very happy that they've managed to find jokes from the set-ups I gave them. So now we just need to learn how to find the set-ups ourselves! This means learning to read in a different way. Take the gag about the Queen staring at the ceiling of the Sistine Chapel. The newspaper that this quote came from probably said something like:

> *They toured many of the ancient treasures the city had to offer. The Queen spent a long time staring at the ceiling of the Sistine Chapel that was painted by Michelangelo in the 15th century. Prince Philip commented that it was a magnificent...*

So the person who wrote the joke had to read the newspaper line by line and see it as a series of separate phrases, not as a whole sentence, in order to isolate those words and play off them.

Similarly, the person who wrote the gag about the Californian fires probably had to pluck the line, *They had to douse the fire with whatever they could get their hands on,* from the middle of a tragic report about people trying to save their homes from the ravages of fire. It might be ruthless, but if you are a joke writer it's what you have to do. I hand out a photocopied article from the newspaper and set the next exercise.

EXERCISE 8: FINDING SET-UPS

Read this article *twice* and pick out the lines that might make good set-ups. You don't have to write a joke straight away you are just looking for potential. When I do this with my class, I put them in twos and make one of them read it to each other SLOWLY, so their brains can marinate the words.

IT'S SUM TASK TO FIND A NEW CAROL

By Elisa Roche

CHANNEL 4 is set to be inundated by mathematicians after yesterday launching a nationwide search to find the next Carol Vorderman.

The station is looking for a man or woman of any age with 'charm and charisma' to appear on the quiz show Countdown from January 2009. Vorderman, 47, announced in July that she would step down from the show after 25 years, saying she had refused to accept a 90% pay cut. Interested applicants – who must have 'excellent' numeracy and literacy skills – can apply via the Channel 4 website from today. Short-listed applicants will be invited to attend televised auditions in October and November. The closing date for applications is September 19. Vorderman was part of the original team on the words and numbers quiz – the first programme broadcast when Channel 4 began in 1982. She quickly won a large fanbase as the pretty maths expert and became a sidekick to late presenter Richard Whiteley. Countdown's current host, Des O'Connor, has said he will leave the show in November after presenting more than 500 editions. His replacement will be announced later this year.

O'Connor and Vorderman will be honoured with a Christmas farewell special. Meanwhile, Vorderman is rumoured to be writing a tell-all book about her years on the show. The show is very popular.

Troubled singer Amy Winehouse recently told OK! magazine that she was a huge fan of the quiz. Producers are said to have offered the star an 'open invitation' to appear as a celebrity guest on the new series when it airs next year.

The most interesting lines are...

....

....

....

....

....

....

....

They are interesting because...

....

....

....

....

....

....

....

....

....

(this gives you a chance to explore your lines and their joke potential)

HOW DID THE CLASS DO?

Again, there are no right or wrong answers. I once did this exact exercise at a conference with fifty people, and almost every line had been chosen by someone. It's about different brains seeing different things. My class have picked out their most interesting lines, and we discuss how we might play off them. Look at the lines you have chosen, and do the same.

INUNDATED WITH MATHEMATICIANS

What might that be like? Loads of corduroy, glasses and dandruff? How many exactly? They'll know how many are there. Some of them were eating Pi.

THEY ARE LOOKING FOR A MAN OR WOMAN
OF ANY AGE WITH 'CHARM AND CHARISMA'

An obvious gag might be: who might be ruled out by the charm and charisma requirement? Heather Mills, Gordon Brown, The Chancellor of the Exchequer (but that's because he doesn't know enough maths).

MEANWHILE, VORDERMAN IS RUMOURED
TO BE WRITING A TELL-ALL BOOK ABOUT
HER YEARS ON THE SHOW

She is writing it very slowly, she's starting with a vowel, then a consonant, then another vowel.

TROUBLED SINGER AMY WINEHOUSE
RECENTLY TOLD OK! MAGAZINE THAT
SHE WAS A HUGE FAN OF THE QUIZ

(Almost everyone had picked this line out!)

She sits at home watching Countdown, shouting give me an E, give me an E!

They did pick out a few other lines as well such as Des O'Connor 'presenting 500 shows' and Carol Vorderman's 'large fanbase' but we didn't get jokes from those which is fine, you never know which lines will lead to jokes or not.

Now you can see how it's done you are ready to write jokes of your own.

EXERCISE 9: WRITING YOUR OWN TOPICAL JOKES

This is a three stage process so don't panic if you don't write jokes straight away.

1) CHOOSE A SUBJECT OR SUBJECTS

The best subjects are the ones everyone is talking about OR the one that fits perfectly with your act/cartooning skills/sketch characters.

You need a subject that has lots written about it if you are going to get a good crop of gags. More obscure stories need to be easily explainable, such as: The Queen visited Google last week

2) FIND EVERY ARTICLE YOU CAN ON IT

Go on the net, go through newspapers, cut them out. Find the newspaper that has the most details on your subject rather than the paper you prefer reading (even if you have to explain to your friends why you're reading it!)

3) READ EVERYTHING YOU FIND ON YOUR SUBJECT AT LEAST TWICE

Read it once for content and then several times to study every connotation of each sentence. Then:

- Highlight interesting words, phrases with your highlighter pen.
- Highlight words you might be able to do a redefinition on.
- Highlight anything you have an emotional reaction to.

You are looking for anything that takes you away from the main subject and gives your mind something to work with and your brain something to play off.

Your article should now be dotted with colour like a mad mosaic, inconsistent but very pretty.

Read the articles again, looking only at what you have highlighted.

Ask yourself why they are interesting, and try to add detail. Play off words. Even do a mini joke-web on the words and phrases if possible. Remember how long you thought about the examples I gave out earlier before you found the gag. Give these lines the same amount of thought. Have a break from it. Go back to it. Give your background processing brain a chance to work.

CHOOSING THE RIGHT NEWSPAPER

Obviously, these days, there are articles on the net, blogs and downloads which can be just as important. Although I do like a good old fashioned newspaper. Tabloids are good for articles about celebrities but are too short on serious news stories. Mid-ranking papers such as The Express and The Daily Mail love giving their readers salacious details, which are great for writing jokes. The broadsheets are good for political stories, and the weekend broadsheets are also good on getting new angles and details on any news stories, as they are often rehashing the week's output.

HOW DID THE CLASS DO?

Some people love this way of writing as it is very analytical and methodical, and if you are prepared to sift through words and phrases until you find something, you are *guaranteed* to write jokes. Others have found it very difficult to keep concentrating. One person didn't find anything to highlight. (It happens, see troubleshooting for more on this.)

Here is some of the class's work.

OLYMPIC CHAMPION

'The human dolphin, Rebecca Adlington, plans to celebrate her medal win by going on a cruise with her boyfriend.'

Yes, human dolphin goes on a cruise...

Well, the boyfriend's going on the ship and she's going to swim along beside.

'Human dolphin, Rebecca Adlington, admits she's afraid of the sea.'

Obviously she's worried about getting caught in the tuna nets?

MADONNA AND GUY RITCHIE SPLIT

'They have thrown in the towel apparently...'

...but they are still arguing over the plates and crockery.

'Apparently, Madonna goes to bed covered in cream wearing a plastic bag...'

There's no truth to the rumour that the housekeeper once used her to ice a cake.

ICELANDIC BANK COLLAPSES
TAKING BRITISH PEOPLE'S SAVINGS

'This is the country that, in summer, has 24 hour days...'

That will give them more chance to look for our money.

POLITICS

'Gordon Brown famously said, "no more boom and bust"...'

There's certainly no more boom and now he's got rid of the women from the cabinet there's not much bust either.

'President Obama has been seeking ex-president Clinton's advice on how to be a good president...'

So there'll be no Cuban cigars and definitely no chatting to the interns.

SCIENCE

'The Large Hadron Collider has been built to drive particles round at high speed and crash them into each other...'

It cost millions but you could have got a woman to drive and they'd've crashed soon enough.

ROYAL FAMILY

'Camilla Parker Bowles supporters stress how natural she is...'

And I thought she had plastic surgery to look like that!

I think that's a good crop of jokes, so I hand out the troubleshooting guide and move on to the next subject.

TROUBLESHOOTING

Question: Are there any tricks for staying objective when reading articles?

Answer: The best of us can find that hard, especially if it's a juicy story! Unfortunately staying objective is the whole point of this exercise. When the general public read a newspaper they don't find themselves writing gags, but we do, because that's our intention. Reading the article slowly and out loud will help. If you're working near others and don't want to be the nutter, try reading the article over and over again. It should have the same effect. When I do this by the third or fourth reading my brain is so bored with the overall meaning that it's only too pleased to look for interesting asides. If I have to tackle a difficult story because I have been given that subject, I read everything I can find so I get lots of different angles on the same story. I once had to write about the European Exchange Rate Mechanism for a radio show. I read a three page broadsheet article about it over and over again until I found the line.

'Once countries are in they can't pull out.'

I was able to write the joke:

'Which is obviously upsetting Catholic countries.'

I'd managed to do a sex joke about the European Union – but hey, that's my skill!

Question: I'm reading objectively but can't find any lines to highlight. Any tips?

Answer: First of all well done for reading objectively. I once had someone in my class who

101

hadn't written any jokes and so I asked to see what lines he had highlighted. He hadn't got any! He couldn't tell me there was a whole newspaper without a single interesting line so he must have been judging things too soon. Secondly, if a subject is very difficult don't just look for whole lines, look for individual words too. Concentrating on words can really help you change the original meaning of the overall sentence.

If in doubt try this short article below. I have chosen it deliberately because it's a difficult paragraph to write from, I can see TWO words that could have different meanings. How many can you see?

'A London fertility clinic is changing their policy on older mothers as record numbers try to become pregnant after the menopause. As a result two 58 year old women are about to receive treatment. One of the two patients has already been through seven failed IVF cycles.'

The most interesting lines are...

....

....

They could also mean...

....

....

The most interesting words to me were 'Cycles', and 'Policy'.

- 'Cycles' could also mean bikes or washing machines.
- 'Policy' could also mean Insurance Policy.

To turn these into joke ideas:

- IVF cycle sounds like something you get on a washing machine; she had seven IVF cycles, two rinses and a spin.
- I've got a washing machine especially for childless women. It's got an IVF cycle.
- The clinic got a new policy on older mothers; I've got third party fire and theft on mine.

I think out of those ideas the IVF cycle ones are the best (I even tried them out on my friend who has had IVF and she laughed a lot). I couldn't turn the bike idea into anything but I was still right to think about it. It was part of the process.

Problem: I can do the exercises you set but can't do it from a newspaper.

Solution: I won't deny that the exercises I set in class and in this book are cherry picked to make it easy to explain the process. In class, I get you to focus on specific articles whereas when you are faced with a whole newspaper it's easy to get distracted and just flick through and give things a cursory reading. This method works best when you have time and patience (I find I always have the time and patience when I'm being paid and on a deadline!) When I do it, I choose my subject. Then I buy different newspapers than normal in order to get the right one for the subject, I ignore all other articles and focus in on any word or phrase that might take me elsewhere. When I do this in class (I often ask the class to throw me a subject to do while they're doing their work) I mimic this process to good effect to make sure it still works - and it does.

Problem: It seems a lot of effort to go to for a joke that might be irrelevant in a week's time.

Solution: That is, my dear, both the joy and the tragedy of the topical joke writer. So it's your decision about whether they're worth it. If you are writing for topical shows and sketches it's a no-brainer, you have to do it. But also topical gags are brilliant for putting you in the here and now. How clever do you think it looks when something happens in the news at lunchtime and you have a gag, cartoon or sketch about it by that evening? I can tell you it's stunning, but you have to have a basic interest in the news and want to do it. If you are a stand-up you'll find that, although topical jokes have a short shelf life, a lot of them are recyclable. So it's hard at first to drop a gag that you have written about the World Cup, but four years later you can dust it off and update it with the minimum of effort. Also, if you write a joke about a politician having an affair, there's bound to be another politician another time doing the same thing, and you'll be ready. You can build up a bank of jokes you can dip into. You will have a job writing an interesting set that is all topical material (although it has been done when the personality and attitude of the comedian is strong enough). The other drawback is when lots of writers are all concentrating on the latest twist of a news story, there's a greater likelihood that they'll come out with a similar joke to you. (the joke writer's equivalent of two women wearing the same outfit to a party!)

Problem: I like topical jokes but find this method too dry.

Solution: If I have an emotional reaction to a news story then I find it's best to use the Stream-of-Consciousness method of writing, or, for a wacky approach, I do the Surrealist Inquisition. Sometimes I combine this method with the above two methods. I read the newspapers to get the details of the story I want to write about, and feed those into the Stream-of-Consciousness and The Surrealist Inquisition. That way, I cover all bases.

If you are writing for radio and television, they will need unbiased jokes. So even if you do have a rant up your sleeve about the latest political crisis, it might not be relevant, whereas this is a good reliable method of finding jokes. I think it also trains your mind to seek out joke set-ups. It builds up your joke writing muscles. You'll know this has happened when you hear something on the radio or read a headline and immediately think of a punchline.

SUMMARY

Writing jokes from newspapers is about ruthless objectivity, spotting interesting lines and working them until you find the joke.

WHAT'S MOST IMPORTANT: TIME, TENACITY OR TALENT?

Yes, I've got a writing schedule that I stick to. If not I probably wouldn't write at all.

ALAN BENNETT

Recently I was writing jokes for a comic who was doing a corporate gig (see case study in Chapter 15). She sent me the company's blurb, 10 pages of it, all in small print, all an earnest account of the company's doings.

I read it several times and highlighted anything that I thought I could play off and turn into potential joke set-ups. Overnight, I background processed what I'd got, and the next day thought of a few ideas based on the lines I'd highlighted. Pleased with myself, I phoned the comic up. Two hours later she phoned me back to tell me a joke she'd written herself. Interestingly, it was an adaptation of one of my jokes using the same set-up line that I'd got from the company brochure, and I don't mind admitting it was better than the joke I'd come up with for that set-up.

Basically my thinking had set off her thinking. She'd had the company blurb for weeks before she gave it to me but didn't see the set-up.

So who is talented in this scenario? The comic for coming up with a better punchline than me? Or me for finding the set-up?

Many times I've been assigned to write jokes on topics that simply aren't funny...but because I've faced those seemingly insurmountable odds before – and conquered them – I set my schedule, turn on my computer and complete the chore.

GENE PERRET

This happens all the time with my partner. He's a genuinely great help when I'm writing jokes because he always comes out with at least one good gag, but it's always based on set-ups that I have researched and recognised. When I tell him the initial subject, he rarely comes up with anything, but once I have put the work in and got lots of basic ideas, his mind dances the fandango with them. Without me, he draws a blank. I'm the one putting in the time in this scenario.

I admit I'm tenacious and put the hours in to find the set-ups. But isn't tenacity an easier thing to achieve that to be born with talent?

I have another comic friend with a brilliant comic mind. At one time I would slave over writing sketches for hours then phone him up and he would instantly come up with the topper jokes for me. I used to be jealous and wonder why he wasn't writing sketches but he (due to his health) couldn't put the time in.

Perhaps that's how writing partnerships work. One person putting in the broad-based effort, the other topping it up.

I started thinking of myself as the hardworking one. When I thought about joke writing, I would think I can do this because I put the time in. I'm a plodder. Then, when I started teaching joke writing, I realised a wonderful thing. When I looked at students' work I could often see punchlines they couldn't but that were based on their ground-work and set-ups. Suddenly I was being the clever one. I realised that the work has to be done by someone. It just happened that for once it wasn't me.

We actually go into an office every day and we work from eleven until half four, or, if we're feeling particularly creative, until five.

CAROLINE AHEARNE

So where does the real talent lie? Is it thinking of the joke or finding the set-up? There's no definite answer to that but I'll let you ponder it.

Either way, putting in the time looking for potential set-ups and fertile ideas is very important, if only so you can feed them to other people to deliberately stimulate their thinking (and then, if you can, keep the jokes).

No matter how talented you are, unless someone is putting the time in, you're not going to be a prolific joke writer. I've known very talented stand-ups who churn out the same material for years with the occasional new line thrown in. You can get away with it as a stand-up. Sketch and sitcom writers or cartoonists can't.

So what are we really doing when we are putting the time in?

Years ago, when I started out joke writing, putting the time in was the only tool I had. I literally used to sit in front of a computer and type out vague things to do with the subjects I wanted a gag on, and hope for the best. I would sit there until I had done whatever time I had set myself.

Nowadays, I can write a lot faster, because I have tools. I can force angles and ideas out more quickly by using the exercises I teach in this book. People have been so impressed with the speed I can come up with topical jokes they have called me wonderful things which I'm too modest to write here. I admit my brain is attuned to joke writing, but I'm still putting time in. I run the subject through as many of my joke writing methods as appropriate. I like to do at least an hour a day (and more if I'm on a tight deadline). I break it up, do a bit here and a bit there. I allow my brain time in between, to process everything, and hey presto the gags come. In the initial stages, I am looking for ideas and potential set-ups. In the secondary stages, I am following every lead, chasing down every glimmer of a gag, and telling all my ideas to my partner and any friend who'll listen.

My message is that joke writing can seem hard at first but it's great once you've got some ideas. Your brain loves it. You are giving it something to work with. You tell a friend and their brain loves it too, and each brain has its own special take, so that's twice the joke potential.

Maybe that's why TV companies often put writers into groups. In my writing classes I always encourage students to chip in on other people's stuff, but I tell them that any jokes generated are owned by the person whose subject it is, because they're the ones who put in the work. They provided the stimulation for the rest of the class's brains.

If you have built castles in the air, your work need not be lost; that's where they should be. Now put the foundations under them!

HENRY DAVID THOREAU

So I actually love it when people use my set-ups to write better jokes than me. What's more, they love it too. They feel clever. And I let them. They don't know that I was deliberately tickling their brains with my well researched set-ups. They are usually keen to let me keep the jokes, and my partner always tells me to take the credit for them (bless him).

For me, song writing is something I have to do ritually. I don't just wait for inspiration; I try to write a little bit every day.

SEAN LENNON

None of us likes drudgery. They say great detectives spend a lot of time sifting through stuff, ruling stuff out and I recognise that process when I'm writing jokes.

That's not to deny talent. I could always write jokes, in my slow, lumbering way. I was always witty with friends. Doing it to order, though, or doing it to make a living, requires time and tenacity as well.

SUMMARY

Question: What's the most important thing Time, Tenacity or Talent?

Answer: All of them! Someone's got to put the work in, is it going to be you?

WRITING AS STREAM—OF—CONSCIOUSNESS (HOW TO USE YOUR PASSION!)

The passionate are like men standing on their heads. They see things all the wrong way.

PLATO

Yes, but that's great for joke writing!

ME

It's Week Five of the comedy class and it's time to get passionate. The class don't know it yet, though. I haven't arranged the chairs any differently!

'Now we're going to try writing as a Stream-of-Consciousness' I tell them. 'This is the antidote to all my logical ways of writing gags. I'm going to mine your brains for passion, for the reasons you feel that way, and find some humour in it. Because if you care about a subject, it's *fantastic* for comedy.'

The class sit motionless. It's me who's gone all passionate.

'If there is something that irritates you, it will probably irritate others' I shout. 'Even if it doesn't irritate others, and it's just some strange quirk of yours that for whatever reason you find most

113

annoying, then behind that reason there might be a joke or witticism or observation. Stream-of-Consciousness basically means you write or speak on a subject without stopping for a set amount of time. You keep going, saying or writing anything, even repetitive things, angry things, rude things, pushing your thoughts forward into no-man's land.'

Normally, when I teach, I illustrate everything by doing a group example first. But Stream-of-Consciousness writing is an individual pursuit, so I ask for a volunteer who is willing to stand up in front of the group and talk about something they feel passionate about. A brave chap called Steve steps forward and says he will talk about hating people who deny that climate change is man-made. (A few others in the group screw up their faces – we're in for an interesting class.)

'Okay, start to talk about that and look at me if you need a prompt,' I say.[25]

'I hate people who deny climate change is man-made,' he says.

'They get on my nerves, they're pathetic, stupid, short-sighted idiots.'

He looks at me.

'Let it all out!' I encourage him.

He does another 30 seconds of tirade before he dries up.

'They must think...' I shout.

---

[25] This is an edited transcript, dots indicated where I have truncated things...

'They must think they're immune. That the whole world system could collapse and they'll be okay in their little houses in their tiny world. The first time they'll notice that climate change has destroyed the world is when there's nothing on telly. They'll say it's not their fault, they never used to watch the weather. Though you don't have to watch the weather...cos these days the news is *about* the fucking weather, you don't need the news and the weather. The weather is the news.'

This gets a laugh from the class. Steve is pleased but it makes him dry up again. He looks at me for a prompt.

'If I were God...' I say.

'If I was God I would kill them all now.' (This gets a titter from the group.)

'Why wait until the planet is exhausted from trying to supply all their fat-arsed needs. (The student is frothing at the mouth now.)

'It's like a mother trying to feed billions of children on a budget, I mean you can't do it, in fact it is Mother Earth ... (The student compares Mother earth to Mothers for a while before drying up.)

'It's just like...' I prompt.

'It's just like, it's just like...' ('It's okay to repeat it' I shout as he's starting to panic).

'It's just like in the Bible. Doesn't it say this is going to happen? War and pestilence in 2,000 years time, which is now isn't it?... So God kind of planned this. How weird. He knew 2,000 years ago he would be angry with us. There was no incentive for those early people. "Keep this up and you'll be sorry in 2,000 years time."' (The class laugh and he looks at me.)

'In a parallel universe...' I offer.

'In a parallel universe everything in the world is run on wind power and solar panels. Yeah, in the parallel universe they didn't have an industrial revolution, they didn't invent the steam engine, no, so they invented the, er, STREAM engine, powered by rivers." (Steve looks pleased with himself at this. I can see his mind really working now.)

He goes on to talk about the SCREAM engine, powered by screams and the DREAM engine. He does a few minutes on how this would work, how the screamers and the dreamers would be wired up etc, then he looks at me again.)

'What really gets to me...'

'What really gets to me is that people who deny climate change just can't see the bigger picture. They're small minded bigots, seeing only their own little lives. They can't see the bigger picture,' he repeats, 'despite the fact they've got 52-inch tellies.' (This gets a big laugh.)

'I want to sit and write that down,' he says.

'It's all right we've got it on tape' I reply. Try again with 'what really gets to me.'

He starts again. 'What really gets to me is that we haven't done anything about this before because big business need to lead it.' (He does a few more lines on this before he comes out with...)

'We ought to make Mother Earth PLC. And charge everyone for using her resources and everyone on the planet are her shareholders... Actually I think big business are a bit worried cos they've realised most of the oil is hidden underneath countries that pathologically hate them. Mind you if we go solar, most of the sun is above countries that pathologically hate them.'

The class laugh. Steve looks at me pleadingly so I tell him it's okay to stop.

He's done his 10 minutes. His face is flushed but he looks happy.

That's what happens when you keep talking. And it works the same if you keep writing. You just need to write or talk without stopping and it doesn't matter whether it's funny, you're processing ideas at a rapid speed and pushing them out, the more you push out the more ideas follow. Not only that, if you look at it or listen to it the next day, you can extend your ideas and use your own lines as set-ups the way we did in *Writing From Newspapers* (Chapter 7).

I ask the class if anyone else wants to try.

'Yes, me,' says a bloke at the back.

'What's your subject?'

'I hate people who whinge on about climate change all the time.' Everyone laughs.

We do a few more, and I tell them to try it for homework as a written exercise, and hand out the following question sheets:

- *Stream-of-Consciousness: Basic Questions*
- *Stream-of-Consciousness: Things You Secretly Love or Hate*
- *Reverse Stream-of-Consciousness*

HOW TO DO STREAM-OF-CONSCIOUSNESS

Choose a topic. It's usually best to focus on the people or organisation behind whatever it is that irritates you. So don't choose adverts, choose the people who make them. It's not the trains themselves, it's the people who run the train company.

Write for 10 minutes on your topic. Start with 'It irritates me because...' and write as much as you can. When you dry up, look at the prompts over the page. Copy each prompt out and continue to write. The most important thing is to keep going, to push through.

Turn off your internal censor, be prepared to be repetitive, just keep writing for the set amount of time.

Have a break and then read it through, see if you can pick up on anything. Can you take anything further? Can you use the statements that you have made as a basis for word-play, the way we did in *Writing From Newspapers*? Could you joke-web some of the ideas?

EXERCISE 10: STREAM-OF-CONSCIOUSNESS (BASIC QUESTIONS)

They must think ...

If I was God I would ...

The next thing they will be doing is ...

It would be poetic justice if ...

It's just like ...

In a parallel universe ...

What's really ridiculous is ...

If I could change just one thing ...

What really gets to me is ...

The one thing I want to say to them is ...

If they were members of my family ...

EXERCISE 11: STREAM-OF-CONSCIOUSNESS (THINGS YOU SECRETLY LOVE OR HATE)

We all love hearing secrets as long as they are other people's. We can use this for our comedy, although, as one of my students said, 'If we tell you what we secretly love and hate it won't be a secret anymore.'

Yeah, but think how much better you'll feel!

I secretly love/hate ...

It makes me feel ...

It's really good / bad because ...

I don't want people to know because ...

People who do this are ...

When I'm pretending the opposite I feel ...

EXERCISE 12: REVERSE STREAM-OF-CONSCIOUSNESS

Don't worry! Learning to reverse a Stream-of-Consciousness is not like learning to reverse a car. Basically, this is an exercise in advanced sarcasm. Whatever you love, you pretend you hate, and vice versa. This won't work with everything. It has to be fairly obvious that it's the opposite. For example, I love it when big cars drive past me in the rain and splash me.

I love / hate ...

It makes me feel ...

It's really good /bad because ...

People who do this are ...

The best / worst thing about it is ...

Without it we'd be ...

In a parallel universe ...

HOW DID THE CLASS DO?

You'll notice that the jokes below seem a lot more personal than the ones written using any of the other joke writing methods. The Stream-of-Consciousness does tend to lead to a rant, which is great for stand-up comedy or for putting words into the mouths of sitcom or sketch characters. You can also play 'high-status and superior' with this kind of material. In justifying why you are passionate about something you can despair of the audience (or other characters) for not feeling passionate about it too, and try to wind them up.

This came from the basic Stream-of-Consciousness sheet...

> *I'm telling you he's an idiot. In a parallel universe where every single thing was different - he'd still be an idiot.*

This came from the reverse – very angry – Stream-of-Consciousness sheet...

> *I love having noisy neighbours. I don't need an alarm clock anymore, they helpfully bang on the wall at five EVERY morning. I sometimes wish I was in a parallel universe where I'm the one disturbing them, but then I realise it wouldn't happen 'cos I'd be dead, 'cos nobody else would put up with that shit!*

This idea came from the basic Stream-of-Consciousness sheet, but then the student deliberately worked on looking at the differences in the two celebrities' achievements...

I was upset that Farrah Fawcett's death was overshadowed by Michael Jackson's. I know people think he was the 'King of Pop' and she just did her hair.

He may have spent six hours a day rehearsing the moonwalk but that's how long it took her to get that flick.

This came from the basic Stream-of-Consciousness sheet...

I hate the L'Oreal 'Cos I'm worth it' ads. I'd like to fly to the States just to slap one of those women round the face and when she says 'Why d'you do that?' say 'Cos you're worth it!'

This came from the Secret Love or Hate sheet...

Who here secretly loves their pet so much that you wish it would become human so you can have sex with it?

That bloke over there's thinking 'Why wait until it's human!'

The basic idea came from writing about hating women's magazines but the ideas were worked on afterwards...

> *I hate women's magazines. They offer you the world on the cover and don't deliver. I saw this one that said 'New You, New Look, New Life' That turned out to be an article about the Witness Protection Program. I saw this other one that went 'You Won't Recognise Yourself!' That was an article about Alzheimer's.*

This came from the basic Stream-of-Consciousness that was done in the class example earlier. The student went away and listened to the tape and worked on it...

> *It's funny they always put the weather on after the news, even when the news is about the weather. Yesterday on the news it said there are hurricanes here, rain and flooding there, tomorrow there's the worst snow for 50 years. And then they say, 'and here's the weather' and you think, yeah, I wonder what the weather's like?*

Again, this came from the basic Stream-of-Consciousness exercise done in class...

> *Mother Nature really needs to be more like a real mother. My mum goes, 'have you cleaned your room?' and I go 'yeah!' Mother Nature goes, 'and what about the oil spill in Mexico have you cleaned that up yet?'*

This came from the Secret Love or Hate question sheet...

I secretly love pooing. I keep it secret, cos, well, it doesn't look good on your CV does it?

TROUBLESHOOTING

Question: I've done three sheets. Why haven't I got any jokes?

Answer: It might be that this method is just not for you, but before you give up, go back and look at the sheets you did.

Even if you didn't come up with a joke straight away (which often happens) your thoughts from the perspective of the next day or the day after that are often infinitely interesting. There might be a wealth of starting points in the form of phrases and potential ideas, even if there are no actual jokes yet.

Question: Do you think this is best as a written or verbal exercise?

Answer: Verbally is really powerful if you have someone there to shout prompts at you and write down what you say. It will help if you are sufficiently afraid of this person to keep going when you don't want to and sufficiently confident with them that you don't mind them hearing all your unfunny thoughts in the search for gems. Another writer is ideal for this role as you can take turns. I do however do this at home in my bedroom, just me and a piece of paper, scribbling furiously. I find the key is to keep pushing myself to answer the questions and like I said above, read it through later.

SUMMARY

Writing as a Stream-of-Consciousness is about keeping your thoughts moving, pushing them along, writing or saying *anything* as long as you keep writing.

Using the prompts will get your thoughts out of a rut and into comedic creativity.

NEVER BE ASHAMED OF YOUR JOKE WRITING PROCESS

Great ideas are even better when you share them.

LOESJE

I'm told that in the BBC writers room you can say anything you like and not be judged. It's a haven for the joke writing brain that needs to sift through every connotation without being hampered by other people's judgement. Everyone there knows joke writing is a process. Everyone accepts that they're going to say some great things, some rubbish things, some obscure things, some weird things - it's all fine.

One writer told me that when he's in brainstorming sessions with other writers, the most important thing for him is to just say something. If he starts to clam up, he's lost. His brain freezes. If he says something, anything, it loosens him up and makes him part of the team.

I know this from when we were recording the topical panel show *The Treatment*. We were expected to chip in on all the subjects, not just the ones we'd been assigned. I found that as long as I had some kind of comment (the weakest of jokes would do) someone else would often pick up on it. I would be part of the conversation, and once you've made one comment it's easier to make the next.

I practice this philosophy on my joke writing courses. If students seem reluctant to talk then I give them the following speech.

'No matter how rude an idea you have, I have written something ruder. No matter how politically incorrect your thought is, I thought something worse. No matter how weak a joke you have written I have written something weaker. You need to let all thoughts and ideas out of your system, because if you don't they'll stick in your mind like a train stuck in a station and other thoughts won't be able to get through. Think of it as a train of thought...'

> *To live a creative life, we must*
> *lose our fear of being wrong.*
> JOSEPH CHILTON PEARCE

Even so some students can still look a bit disappointed if I say something that is clearly unfunny rubbish. I can see them thinking, 'Blimey! She's the teacher, she should do better than that.'

And I *can* do better than that. I can do worse as well. I have no control. I just let it all come tumbling out. I say rubbish things, I say obscure things, I say puns a child of five could have written, and I say great things, but I needed to say all the other things to get there. So when students look at me that way I say: this is the process. Often, to write one good joke, you have to write a number of mediocre jokes, and before that a lot of half jokes and even more non jokes and ideas that you're not sure what to do with.

Don't be ashamed of your methods. Don't worry about the half jokes and non jokes. Don't shrink away and think they are crap, and therefore decide it means you're crap. NO, it's part of the process. You are on your way to a fabulous joke. If you shut down the process, you shut down your thinking and you shut down your own potential. This especially applies when you are working with someone else. If they say something and you say 'Naaa, that's rubbish mate,' they're never going to say anything again. But if you take their idea and think about it, you might be able to add to it or do a twist on it. It becomes part of the flow of ideas.

There is the risk that you cannot afford to take, (and) there is the risk you cannot afford not to take.

PETER DRUCKER

I once had a student in my class who was very loud, bossy and critical. When I put students into groups to work, I would hear her saying 'Nope, nope,' until her team would be sitting in silence afraid to speak. During one of the sharing sessions she confided that she often invited people round her house to write with her.

'They come round once and I don't see them again' she said.

I think she was lucky to get someone round once!

I'm glad my friends are not like her. If ever I try my jokes out on them I always start by saying that some of them are rubbish, some are okay, some are half-formed but 'I'm going to read them all because I believe that's what you have to do in the joke writing process,' and they nod solemnly while I go through everything.

There's always one joke I hate and they love and vice versa; they'll always make one comment that leads me to another thought and another joke and there are always the duds that don't work - but in the bigger scheme of things it doesn't matter.

We used to never say 'no' to each other, if we didn't like each other's idea we'd just stay silent. Sometimes we were silent for so long we forgot what we were being silent about.

GALTON AND SIMPSON

None of that could happen if I followed my prejudices and prejudgements – and I do have them. I just live with them. I even send off ideas that I'm not sure about, because you never know what others will make of things.

Some people I know are so self-critical they won't even write something down in their notebook, let alone tell it to anyone, which is crazy, because, you know what? It doesn't matter if you have a *hundred* unworthy sentences written down if it leads to one joke. It's not a testimony about your personality. No-one's going to read it at your funeral as a measure of who you were, so write it down and let it go, or try and adapt it. See *Honing* (Chapter 13).

Here's the news: creativity is a process. Creative people are simply better at running this process (whether they do it consciously or not) than their less creative (and slightly more envious) peers.

JOE GREGORY

So don't judge anything. See everything as part of the joke writing process. If necessary, tell yourself that you will burn all your notes, but I have to tell you that I used to keep all mine because sometimes you don't see the joke until long after you have written it. I would often go through all my old notes on a joke hunt and would be pleasantly surprised. The joy of distance: leave something long enough and you will have forgotten that you wrote it, then you will really see what's funny and what isn't.

SUMMARY

Sharing ideas is one of the most powerful joke writing tools we have. It's probably good for the soul too!

THE SURREALIST INQUISITION (COMING AT A SUBJECT FROM WEIRD & WONDERFUL ANGLES)

To raise new questions, new possibilities, to regard old problems from a new angle, requires creative imagination and marks real advance in science.

ALBERT EINSTEIN

...and joke writing.

ME

It's nearly the end of the course and time to string the students up and ask them some strange questions: It's the Surrealist Inquisition! Weirdies, beardies and profound thinkers love this method of writing jokes. It's for finding new angles on old, well-worn subjects. It's for shaking up the way you think and coming at things from somewhere else completely. When I tell my students this, they look pleased, especially the surrealists - I do have some, they live in the fish tank at the back of the room and blow bubbles at me!

'But,' I say, 'The Surrealist Inquisition takes more thought than the other methods and I'm not being sarcastic when I say for some people that's hard.

I'm going to put a series of questions to you. And your initial response might be to draw a blank: 'Nothing fits. Nothing works. What's the point, Sally?' So I need you to humour me. Go through the motions, try to answer the questions and see what happens.'

The students look a bit scared now.

'This is an exercise in fitting square pegs into round holes and the resulting push is where the creativity happens.'

I get out my *Surrealist Inquisition Question Sheet* and we choose the subject of democracy, which is broad, well-worn and, to be honest, a bit humdrum. Lovely.

I read them the first question...

'Describe democracy to aliens.'

'The mass of the people voting for their leaders,' ventures my first brave student.

'Breakdown the words "voting" and "people",' I say. 'Aliens won't understand that.'

'The beings on our planet register their opinion about who should lead them.'

'Good,' I say. 'Now imagine you're aliens watching the beings on our planet register their opinion about who should lead them. What might they think?'

'That it's cumbersome,' says the bloke next to me. 'Some alien species don't need elections. They can just read everyone's mind and know what to do.'

'Okay, apply that back to us and our democracy,' I say.

'If it was like here we'd have Uri Geller as President of the world,' he replies.

'Or Derren Brown, says another student,' screwing up her face.

This is a great idea, and for the next five minutes the class chat excitedly about what it would be like having a mind-reader or illusionist running the country. They discuss how it would affect Prime Minister's Question Time and whether they would end it by saying, 'Was that your card?' Election broadcasts might start: 'Look into my eyes, look into my eyes.'

I tell them this is ideal for a double joke-web on illusionists and political leaders. I'm pleased we've got a good solid idea, and we're only on the first question! I read them the next one...

'How is democracy different in other countries?'

We kick around the idea of communist states, and don't get anywhere. I tell the class it's okay, because we have explored it and now we can move on. I know people are always uncomfortable when things seem not to work, but when you are searching for comedic ideas, not everything does.

It's like looking for the teabags in a strange kitchen. You have to open all the drawers and cupboards before you track them down.

'What do other countries do? Think about extreme opposites to us?'

'In theocracies, the leader is chosen by God,' says one student.

'Apply the leader being chosen by God to democracy,' I say.

He thinks for a while.

'Well, I suppose God's the only member of the electorate,' he says, smiling, 'Do you think they set up a polling station for him and canvas His vote?'

'Surely God would literally be a floating voter,' someone else says.

We all laugh at that, and the panic that we didn't find anything on communist states is over, as the ideas flow fast from the students.

'They're assuming there's only one God. What about the Greek and Roman gods. Go to a theocracy and say, "if your election criteria is God, we've got some other Gods here who'd like a vote."'

'The Christian God knows where to put the cross, there must be a pun there?'

'Buddha would more likely be the floating voter,' says someone else who's clearly been thinking about it. 'He'd be rising above it all.'

The class are now on a roll. I let them finish and read them the next question...

'Describe the situation to a child in terms they can understand. Put yourself in their place and imagine how they would respond?'

The class start describing democracy in terms of the X Factor but we realise that this idea is in the popular consciousness now anyway.

Are there any other parts of the voting process we can explain to a child?

'What about the manifesto?' someone says.

'Try it.'

'They have what's called a manifesto where the people who want to lead us set out what they are going to do.'

'Okay, think about that from the child's point of view.'

'If I didn't know the word manifesto,' says one student, 'I would think it was the name of a pizza in an Italian restaurant. Antipasti, manifesto, linguine.' Everyone loves this.

'Yeah, politicians don't stick to the manifesto, they have pasta as well.'

'Wonderful,' I say. We kick around the idea of school timetables being a manifesto but it doesn't go anywhere so we move on to the next question...

'Find an analogy.'

Nobody responds. 'Usually, finding an analogy is one of the hardest parts of the Inquisition' I say and show the class some previous examples.

We all know chaos theory is usually described as a butterfly flapping its wings in Brazil causing a hurricane elsewhere.

If you have been doing the Surrealist Inquisition on this subject, you will have already broken it down to explain it to both aliens and small children. So you could've got down to the basic kernel that Chaos Theory is where something really small can turn into something big, something small can have big consequences. Once you have got the penis gags out the way (!) you trawl through your mind and look for other things to which you can apply those criteria:

For example when chaos theory was first popularised in the early nineties, comedienne Jenny Vickers came out with the joke...

> *I know chaos theory's true, because one day my Dad farted and the next day the Berlin wall came down.*

This has kept to 'tiny' and 'enormous' criteria. Here's a couple I wrote...

> *Chaos theory, where something small can turn into something large? Yeah one day I ate this tiny little cake and the next day my bum was enormous.*

> *Chaos theory: like a tiny remark to your mum that you saw your dad giving mouth to mouth resuscitation to his secretary and the next day they have a massive row.*

That's three different analogies for one theory and I'm sure there are more. These ideas won't jump into your head. You have to break the idea down to its simplest form and then think hard about what you can apply it to. Outside of class I often go for a walk in order to think of an analogy, simply because I know one might not come straight away and I might as well have some nice scenery while I'm thinking! But back in class they are ready to start again.

'So we can try and find an analogy for democracy or any of the things that make up democracy.'

'I'm still thinking about the manifesto,' says the quiet woman in the corner who doesn't say much normally.

'Break Manifesto down to its basic kernel,' I say.

'It's where you state what you are going to do before you do it.'

'Good, so is there an analogy for that?'

'What about if we had to have a sexual manifesto? Where people have to tell you what they're going to do before you go to bed with them?' This gets a chuckle from the class.

'And also what they are not going to do,' says the bloke next to her, leaning forward.

'But then people will say that they're going to do stuff and then go back on their word. Just like some politicians,' she replies.

'But if you had their manifesto you could send Jeremy Paxman round to interview them and find out why.'

The group are starting to talk over each other now. One even starts doing an impression of Jeremy Paxman, saying 'It says here you'll kiss for 10 minutes and not less.'

The class have got the point about analogies so we move on to the next question...

'Think about it from the point of view of any objects, places or people that are directly or indirectly involved.'

'If you want to be surreal, choose an object and think about it from the object's point of view,' I add. Again, it's a while before anyone speaks.

'How about the ballot box?' says one chap.

'Okay, imagine you are a ballot box, you're only brought out occasionally and you're stuffed full of papers and then emptied.'

'Sounds like bulimia to me.' (The quiet woman from earlier is now definitely on a roll[26]). 'They get nothing for ages and then they are stuffed full of ballot papers, that's an eating problem if ever I heard of one.'

'Can you imagine putting your vote in the ballot box and it burps,' says someone else.

'That would make a great cartoon,' I say. 'Any other objects or people?'

'Where do all those pens come from on election day?' says the same person who came up with ballot box. 'I reckon they co-opt them from the bookies or Argos for one day's service. These pens normally spend their time making bets or buying rubbish but for one day these pens get to choose the government.'

I'm impressed at his thinking.

---

[26] When I teach the Surrealist Inquisition Question Sheet there is always at least one person who has usually been quite quiet throughout the course who suddenly comes to life.

'Did that idea just pop into your head?' I ask.

He looks a bit embarrassed but says, 'To be honest I couldn't think of anything so I imagined an election, going to the polling station, seeing the ballot box, seeing the pens.'

'Basically you're thinking about it,' I say. 'It sounds obvious, but there's no reason why we should think of everything off the top of our heads. It's a myth that joke writers are all geniuses. Talk to any of them and they'll tell you a lot of it is drudge work, sifting through stuff, but once you get an idea it's really exciting, and you do look really clever, which is what you look like right now.'

The chap beams at me.

'I cannot overstate how much thinking the Surrealist Inquisition takes, but you get such a good crop of gags that it's so worth it.'

I hand out the Question Sheets (see Exercise 13) and set them the homework of choosing a subject for the Surrealist Inquisition to interrogate.

EXERCISE 13: THE SURREALIST INQUISITION QUESTION SHEET

Think really hard about each question. If you find yourself going off at a tangent, that's good. Just remember to apply the ideas back to the main subject.

Describe the situation to aliens... *Don't say 'lotion', say 'white sticky stuff' – talk in alien speak, then think about the same situation from the alien point of view, looking down on what is happening.*

How is this situation different in other countries?
Think of the most extreme opposite practice of another country that you can.

Describe the situation to a young child...
Put it in terms they can understand. Put yourself in the place of the child and imagine how they would respond to what's being said.

See if you can find an analogy? *Break the situation down to its basics and think of other things that are the same. If you're stuck try finding an analogy in how tribal societies do things or in the animal world.*

Think about it from the point of view of any objects or things or people that are directly or indirectly involved...

HOW DID THE CLASS DO?

I love this. Some of the class who never had a surreal thought in their lives were tempted into the weird zone! I have included clever ideas that I loved as well as the jokes, just so you can see the range of output. Underneath each idea, I have put how it was generated by the questions.

The problem with ageing is that your skin keeps getting bigger and wrinkly but your bones don't. If only our skulls would keep getting bigger too it would take up the slack and stretch out our skin like an instant face lift.

Obviously our heads would be enormous. The sign that you are older would just be having an enormous head. I could live with that. They'd have to stop calling psychiatrists 'shrinks' though in case we got the wrong idea.

The one great thing about getting old is that you can do the Hokey Cokey – with your teeth. ..

In, Out, In Out, Shake them all about!

(Ageing from the point of view of the objects involved)

It must be hard being an indoor plant on a windowsill – especially if your owner doesn't water you. When it rains you'd see the water coming towards you splattering on the glass but it never gets to you. It must be like torture, in fact it's sort of the opposite of water boarding.

Some indoor plants have a good time though. The plant in my lounge watches telly. Yeah, my plant's a couch potato. Well actually it's a delphinium.

(Thinking about plants from the point of view of the objects involved)

In this country we like to take dogs for a walk, in Korea they take them to a wok.

(Thinking about what they do with dogs in other countries)

When we domesticated dogs we took away their chance to hunt food and run with the pack and instead we have to walk them. Dogs are like: 'There's no point man, what's my motivation here?'

(Thinking about dog walking from the point of view of the dog)

I wish we had evolved from chameleons instead of monkeys. That whole colour-changing thing would wipe out racism in a stroke. Although to be fair I don't think chameleons can help which colour they are, they just blend in with whatever's there. So in the countryside we'd be green. On the beach we'd go sandy. And God help us if we went into a house with 70's wallpaper!

(Think of analogy for colour prejudice)

I'm very jealous of the way fish reproduce. They just let their eggs out and other fish come along and fertilise them. How great is that? I'd love to let an egg out onto a leaf and let it be fertilised. Actually I'd be much better off leaving my egg on a porn mag. Much more of a chance that there's going to be some sperm coming along there.

(Thinking about an analogy for reproduction in the animal world)

What's this? Living things crammed into a tiny space and forced to travel for long distances, unable to breathe. Live animals being transported to Europe? Or your feet in those high heels madam?

(Thinking about wearing high heels from the point of view of the feet)

TROUBLESHOOTING

Problem: I get what you're doing but when I tried it nothing happened.

Solution: The Surrealist Inquisition can be tough! If you're struggling, the best way to get into it is to go through the motions. When you're asked to describe the situation to aliens, actually do it. Be like the aliens in the Cadbury's Smash advert - if you're old enough to remember them. They describe potatoes like this: They boil them for 20 of their minutes then they smash them all to pieces. Try it like that. Then see yourself as an alien looking at your subject. Every time you go off at an angle, apply it back to the subject, the way we did in the group exercise. Then imagine a child you know and explain it to them. Imagine what they might make of it.

Do this for ALL the questions. Accept that some of them might not work but, if you have done it thoroughly, at least you have ruled out that avenue. The student who wrote the jokes about plants in the *How Did The Class Do?* section told me that explaining gardening and plants to a child didn't yield anything and that the act of gardening is often used as an analogy, so the analogies section didn't go very well either.

But, and this is the important bit, other parts of her Inquisition did work. For the aliens section she imagined the aliens were Triffids judging how we treat our plant life here with pesticides and being very cross about it. Then when she started thinking about things from her indoor plant's point of view, thinking about it not being watered and there being water outside the window, and thinking about it watching telly, then it all started happening.

Question: Could you use this method without the aim of being surreal?

Answer: You could indeed. For example, when I did Democracy with a class, a student described the British Houses of Parliament as 'a place where people go and argue about what to do.'

And another student said 'I call that home,' which got a big laugh[27]. The student was playing off the

---

[27] I didn't use it in the original example because I can't include everything from the classes.

unusual way we are describing things, using it as a set-up as we do in other joke writing methods.

To do it this way, write out your answers to the surrealist inquisition, have a break and then study the lines the way you would study a newspaper or magazine looking for jokes. The difference being that these should be way out there wacky ways of looking at things which should help bring home those lines.

SUMMARY

Surrealist comedy is often about looking at things from unusual angles, use the question sheet to take your thinking to weird and wonderful places.

Why not try it to find new jokes about hackneyed subjects?

ALWAYS LEAVE ROOM FOR THE MAGIC

That little bit of loose and scruffy freedom, that place between effort and intuition, is where the magic lives.

FRANK SKINNER

It feels magical when jokes just come. You are on a roll or just mulling something over and there it is, a fabulous gleaming beautiful funny joke. And you thought of it. *You*, how clever you are!

But the real magic is what you do with your ideas, all of them, not just the instantly hilarious ones, but the weird ones, the thoughtful ones and the half-baked ones. Spike Milligan was a compulsive joke writer. Anthony Clare called him a 'manic punner', but his real genius was that he didn't just think of a pun and leave it there, he pushed it forward to its ultimate extreme. This is where the magic lies.

The exercises in this book will generate jokes but it's what you do with them that's the real skill.

I love it when someone comes up with an idea and I can't work out how they thought of it! I know they have taken a leap that defies even the crazy logic of joke writing and it thrills me.

149

I was watching a DVD of *Seinfeld.*

It was the episode where Jerry and George end up as passengers in the chauffeur-driven car of a Nazi leader who has been held up at his previous destination. George gets mistaken for the Nazi and comedy magic ensues.

'Wow how did they think of that?' I wondered, so I watched the additional notes about the show. Larry David said that for ages he had up on his whiteboard the idea that they would take the wrong car at the airport. One day it came to him that the car could be that of a Nazi leader.

Lulled in the countless chambers of the brain, our thoughts are linked by many a hidden chain; awake but one, and in, what myriads rise!

ALEXANDER POPE

By leaving that idea on the whiteboard he was leaving room for the magic, allowing passing ideas and fancies to attach themselves to that idea. He was leaving it open, not clamping down on it.

The important thing is that he had an idea. The next important thing is that he wrote it down. Sounds obvious, I know, but so many people don't even bother to write good ideas down, let alone half-baked ones. I know my brain is so pleased when I get any idea that it assumes I will remember it. I know from bitter, bitter experience that it doesn't. Also, by writing things down you are honouring the idea, opening it up to the universe where it can intersect with any passing whims and fancies, and your brain can do a long, slow background process on it. I regularly read through my notebook to check up on how the ideas are simmering, hooking them into my latest ideas. I love the thought of Larry David's white board. It's not surprising that he still one of the most creative people around. He's clearly very open to the process. He leaves ideas to ferment with passing yeasts!

Be patient, be true to yourself, follow your natural inclinations and your God-given talents will reveal themselves to you.

JUDY CARTER

When I give this speech to my classes, someone always asks 'What if you haven't got time, and need to force ideas? What if you are on a deadline?'

In that case I would suggest you try improvising around them and start trying to hone them, see which ones have legs. I also say this in *Honing* (Chapter 13).

In London some comics go to new material nights where you can try out stuff with less pressure. Frank Skinner says he loves the process of ideas evolving during his live performances. He lets their 'improvised additions blossom and grow; to develop dexterity, the certainty of delivery that is honed by repetition, to find its less obvious magical places.'[28]

---

[28] This and other brilliant observations about writing and performing comedy are in Frank Skinner's book *On the Road. Love, Stand-up Comedy and the Queen of the Night.* Random House. 2008

Let ideas ferment and grow, whether fast or slow. There's nothing worse than abandoning an idea and then a year later seeing someone else take it to a place you never dreamt of. So follow that glimmer like the wise men following a star. Add to it, nurture it and let it grow, but, most of all, leave room for the magic. And the thing about magic is you never know where it's lurking.

Doesn't it often seem that when we let go of conscious thinking – that desire to analyse or control the outcome – then we begin to gain access to the vast potential of our unconscious mind that seems to know so much more than we do.

CYGNUS REVIEW

SUMMARY

Some ideas take a long time to ferment and come to fruition and that's okay, they will be deeper and richer for it. Why not go through your old note books and open up those old ideas to your latest thinking?

HONING

The difference between a joke working or not is sometimes just down to some indefinable turn of phrase.

DAN EVANS

It's lovely towards the end of a joke writing course, sitting in front of a room full of joke writers. They know how to break-up words, do joke-webs and trawl newspapers for interesting lines. They can use their passion for subjects to find jokes and finally they know how to get surreal. The class always generates loads of ideas but, as I said in the previous chapter, turning them into routines, sketches, lines in sitcom, there lies the magic and perhaps the genius. In every other part of the course I try to give out formulas and exercises. Do this, do that, there's your joke.

I can't do that with honing. It's too individual. Plus I don't want to tell anyone what style they should be doing their comedy in. So all I do is give a bit of a lecture which I will recreate here and look at jokes that have already been honed.

So the first rule of honing is that there are no rules, only guidelines and they're contradictory.

If I had to choose my three favourite honing guidelines they'd be:

1. NEVER THROW AWAY OR TYPE OVER YOUR PREVIOUS VERSIONS OF GAGS

You can't judge what's good until you have distance.

2. ALLOW SPACE FOR THINGS TO FAIL

Your brain will surprise you and will take you and your ideas to the most amazing places if you let it. Give ideas space to breathe. If some jokes end up dying horrible deaths it's so that others can live.

3. WHEN YOU FIND A JOKE WRITE DOWN THE EXACT WORDING IMMEDIATELY

You may never find it again. Jokes can be like a mirage in the desert, a glimmer of truth, like an elusive love that ever more eludes you (yeah right – but ask certain comedy writers and they'll tell you it's so).

Everything else about honing are just things that you can try that may or may not work.

TO FIND OUT IF A JOKE NEEDS HONING...

Say it out loud. If that works, tell it to a friend. If they laugh you're on to a winner.[29]

If, when you start saying your joke out loud, it comes out woolly and you can't even get the set-up right let alone the punchline then what you've probably got is a *joke idea* rather than a joke.

That's when honing comes into its own and you can try any or all of the following on it...

TO FIND THE CENTRAL KERNEL OF A JOKE...

Ask yourself, 'What is it that makes this funny?'

For example a friend of mine wrote a very sick joke about the terrible fire tragedy that was in the news that week. The joke ran that if the survivors of the tragedy had a reunion they'd call it 'Friends Reignited.' He loved his joke but thought people would be offended by it.

I told him that the central kernel of the joke was sound-alike/word play Reignited/Reunited. So this joke doesn't have to be about that particular fire tragedy it can be about anything to do with fire. So we changed it to...

When arsonists have a reunion they call it Friends Reignited.

---

[29] This might seem that I am just referring to stand-up but the writers of Peep Show (Sam Bain and Jesse Armstrong. See *Peep Show The Scripts* - 2006) said they never know if something truly works until they hear the cast say it.

Lovely. No insulting fire tragedy survivors (or their relations) just a nice word play gag.

Basically once you recognise the central kernel you can change the joke as long as you stay true to it.

I was trying to write some jokes for an MP. I won't name the town, let's say he comes from Anytown. The first line I came up with was:

You need someone to represent Anytown which is a bit tatty, run down and problems with drugs, alcohol and underage sex.

Here I am!

Obviously my MP isn't going to say that. It attacks both him and the town he represents. The central kernel of the joke is mistaking the town's problems with his personal problems.

After much thought (I did agonise over this one) I came up with...

I'm MP for Anytown

Wrongly assumed to be a bit tatty, run down, problems with alcohol... But enough about me...

Just by adding the 'wrongly assumed' it takes the sting out of the gag and makes it harmless but hopefully still funny; obviously the 'underage sex' line had to go too!

I once wrote a joke for a student in my stand-up class who was doing an act as a monk. The joke ran:

> *As a monk it can be very difficult going years without sex... But it does help me understand the married men in my congregation.*

The first time he told it like that and it got a laugh. The next time he came to class he changed the wording to:

> *I'm a monk and I'm celibate. Yes I'm celibate, like the married men in the audience.*

It didn't get a laugh. The central kernel of that joke is a play on the words 'go years without sex'. The vague wording allows us to link monks to the supposed frustrations of married men. Saying the word celibate is too strong, it implies a philosophy and commitment and deadens the nuance.

So, when you are honing, always remember to stick to the central kernel (and keep your old versions) because sometimes it's easy to forget what was funny about the joke in the first place.

WHEN THERE ISN'T A CENTRAL KERNEL

Sometimes when you look for the central kernel you might even find out that there isn't one. Don't despair! You might have what I call a 'Glimmer of a Gag' (see Chapter 5 for more examples).

You can see the gag in the distance but you can't quite grasp it. I always open a 'Weak Joke Hospital' in my classes to help such ailing specimens. To resuscitate a weak gag I run the basic idea through another joke writing method – 'Open Gag Surgery'!

If you wrote the joke using a joke-web then put it through *The Surrealist Inquisition* or try doing *Stream-of-Consciousness* on it. If it's a pun do a double joke-web on each half of the meaning. Be like surgeons battling to save the life of the gag, give it the oxygen of brain power, the adrenalin of thought and see what happens. If the joke still dies at least you know you've tried everything and you can lay it to rest, grieve for a while and move on.

IS IT TOO WORDY?

Once you have found the central kernel you need to look at the gag as a whole and see whether it's too wordy. To do this, ask yourself 'what's the minimum that this gag needs to make it work?' I once wrote a joke about a politician that came from a newspaper report:

> *On Tuesday afternoon the Deputy Prime Minister could be spotted in the House of Commons steering the Equality Bill gently through its first reading.*

I added the punchline:

> *She's all right steering as long as she doesn't try and park it.*

The politician had recently been done for parking offences so it was a pertinent gag. However the set-up doesn't trip off the tongue very easily so I changed it to:

> *She's steering a bill through parliament at the moment...*

She's all right steering as long as she doesn't try and park it.

It's easy to get attached to long-winded set-up; especially if it sparked your thinking it can seem sacred. It's not. When students do long-winded routines or sketches in class I always tell them to write out their routine in full. Highlight the bits that are funny. Look at the space in between and cut that down as much as possible.

NOT WORDY ENOUGH?

Having told you that jokes can be too wordy I'm now going to say that some jokes need *more* words – I told you there were no rules! That doesn't mean that you can add any old flannel to your gag.

What gags often benefit from is rhythm and repetition. I once had the fascinating experience of being at the back of a comedy club where the sound was so bad I couldn't hear what the comics were saying. Yet, I could still tell who was funny and where the punchlines were. This, of course, is about the comics' timing. And timing is very much helped by rhythm.

But again, any old rhythm isn't going to do. It needs to be the rhythm of your act, your sitcom character's voice or, if you are a strip cartoonist, the number of boxes you need to fill.

If you see a transcript of actual comedians' acts[30] they are full of repetition, and little add-ons like

---

[30] *The Best Stand-up and Comedy Routines* edited by Mike O'Brien (Constable and Robinson) 2006 has transcribed a number of famous modern comic routines.

'you know', and 'yes really', that hold up the punchline or the starting of the next gag.

When Frankie Howard repetitively said, 'ooo don't' and 'yes missus' it was adding to his timing and personality. Or try this one from Arnold Brown:

The best way to lay compost, in my opinion, just in my opinion, is to get someone else to do it.

Brown with his lilting Scottish voice lulls the audience in. If you're not sure try saying it without the 'in my opinion, just in my opinion'. You'll find that it just doesn't have the same rhythm.

Another method is to lull the audience in with a rhythmic list before you hit them with the punchline - this is also called *The Rule of Three*:

Here's one of mine...

I love it that the song 'I Will Survive' is still popular...

It means a whole new generation of women can split up with their boyfriends, learn the words, sing the song, feel the pain and then get back with him anyway.

Can you see where the rhythm is?

Learn the words. Sing the song. Feel the pain.

The words also lead the audience in the opposite direction, so it helps the build up to the punchline.

So once you've honed a joke down you can build it up again according to your or the character's vocal rhythm.

ADDING ATTITUDE

This book is designed to help you write jokes about any subject whether you care about it or not. But if you can muster up an attitude to something it might help you find the right way to present it.

Comedian and writer, Dan Evans, told me that when he's writing for other people, 'It can really help focus if you know they will only want jokes from a perspective that is snide, angry, totally unaware or whatever. Maybe if people are intending to write for themselves they could really try to find what it is about their angle or passion that is very personal to them.'

Even not caring about a subject is an attitude in itself and can help hone your jokes and find the right words for them.

HONING JOKES FOR SITCOMS AND SKETCHES

Sitcoms and some sketches really do rely on the strength of the characters for humour. If the audience get the character they are more likely to get the jokes. If you're not sure about this then re-visit the sitcom *Frasier*. Many of the 'laugh lines' simply aren't jokes at all unless they have his snobbishness behind them - it's quite inspiring. You can, however, still write the jokes first and attribute them after.

One of my students did a joke-web about holidays because he wanted the characters in his sitcom to discuss where they went for theirs. He did a joke-web on whale watching holidays and ended up writing about the Japanese resumption of whaling and juxtaposed the two.

The way he could use this joke idea depends upon the characters in his sitcom. Say he had a character who was a bit tight with money:

'What do you mean I never do anything for you? I took you on that whale watching holiday.'

'Whale Watching? We were the lookout on a Japanese Whaling ship. Every time I spotted a whale they harpooned it!'

Conversely a weak and pathetic sitcom character might end up on a Japanese whaling ship instead of a whale watching holiday and be too polite to say anything...

'Why didn't you say anything?'

'I didn't like to offend them.'

'They caught 26 whales.'

'Yes, I was a strangely good spotter.'

In sitcoms and sketches you can even try getting characters to act out the joke. A character could end up sitting on a Japanese whaling ship in the lookout chair staring sadly out to sea.

So when you are adding jokes to sitcoms and sketches think, 'How would this character react to this?' 'Now what about that character?' and build your scene.

If a character has no attitude to whale slaughter then make that their trait. Why don't they care? Are they too interested in nail polish or computer games? If you don't know the answer then work on it until you do.

Plus you can still use the normal honing rules like *The Rule of Three* (where you can attribute the lines to different characters) and add specific details to help you fit the joke neatly round your characters. Great characters and great jokes make a brilliant sitcom.

HONING JOKES FOR CARTOONS

Cartoons are slightly different from other gags. For a start any stinky old pun that has been beautifully drawn or illustrated is acceptable. Where cartoons are dependent on words to provide the gag then all the same honing tips apply, especially things like *The Rule of Three* because strip cartoons were born for this. I recently did a cartoon for a healthy eating magazine. My basic idea was that most healthy eaters love juicing but never stop complaining about washing up the juicer. I'll admit it's a fairly weak gag. By adding *The Rule of Three* it came out as:

As a cartoon the readers (people who like juicing) get the journey of the juice drinker as well. Cartoons are a lovely way to use the jokes you write and many small magazines use them.

If you think you're not good at drawing – think again. Everyone draws as a child if you haven't drawn for a while it's just going to take you longer. Here's what I do...

- Buy a pad of tracing paper. Use it to draw all your test runs and then choose the best ones and put them together.

- Search on-line for images similar to what you want, trace them to use them as a template and adapt them.

- Buy a small wooden artists doll that you can put into positions to copy for your characters.

- Buy a specialist 'how to draw cartoons' book. There are a number on the market.

So if you have a special interest, such as engineering or cheese making, then there's likely to be a magazine crying out for a cartoonist who can do a gag about it. It's a great way to build up your confidence.

FINAL WORD ABOUT HONING

I know I already said there are no rules but, just to hammer this point home...

A comedy friend of mine used to phone me up on Friday afternoons and tell me the new jokes he'd written. They would sound like utter rubbish to me and the first few times I'd hint that maybe they needed a bit more work. But then I'd see him on stage with that same material getting enormous laughs. Suddenly I could see the funniness, the timing, the big personality and it all came alive. So after that, when I got my Friday afternoon phone calls I would listen to the jokes and say, 'well I bet *you* can make it work!'

So, never forget the first rule of honing.

There are no rules!

There is no other true judge of your work than the audience and they can be fickle. So plough your own furrow, follow your dream, try it this way, or that way, work hard and keep at it.

EXERCISE 14: DIFFERENT WAYS OF SAYING YOUR JOKES OUT LOUD

It can get very boring just reciting your material to yourself so here are some things to try...

- If you imagine a large audience it's easy to think your words aren't good enough. But in fact your large audience is made up of lots of individuals who need to understand the words you are saying. So try saying your joke to one person as in conversation. Play it down, go low key. See how it changes the way you say it.

- Try whispering the joke to someone real or imagined across the room. Whispering is hard so you will naturally hone what you are saying down and give it a different emphasis.

- Imagine you're in a radio studio sitting opposite a presenter. Imagine him asking you questions on the subject and try and drop the gag into your answer. That will show you what you need around the gag.

- If you're hoping to turn your joke into a sketch, start improvising the joke within the sketch, add things to it. Invent characters around it.

- If the joke's going into a stand-up routine try saying it with the gag before and the gag after. Does it need a link line? How does it flow with the other gags? This could lead to you thinking of extra link lines or adding different emphasis.

- Try performing the joke in a foreign accent, strangely this can often help find the right timing or rhythm.

EXERCISE 15: HONING YOUR JOKES

This is a distilled version of everything I have written in this chapter. Go through your notebook picking out *anything* that is vaguely funny. When you find something apply the following prompts to hone it...

- Has the joke got a central kernel? If not try running the idea through another joke writing method to beef it up and find its other funny places.

- Can you add some attitude to the joke? Either your own for stand-up or the characters attitude for sitcom or sketch. Even cartoon characters can have attitude.

- Pare it down to its minimum.

- Try adding rhythm and repetition to it.

- Breathe life into the joke. If it's going to be in a sketch, give the joke to a particular character and start acting it out. If you're a cartoonist start drawing it. If it's going to be in a stand-up routine or monologue, find a place for it in your act and try saying it with the joke that comes before and after it. If you are writing a political speech, add the joke to your text and see if it scans.

- If you don't get it right the first time you hone it, leave it in your notebook and try again another time. You never know what other ideas it might eventually link with.

TROUBLESHOOTING

Question: Why do I have a whole notebook full of half formed jokes and ideas that I can't seem to make work?

Answer: Well if you've really tried to make them work in one medium and can't have you considered finding an outlet in a different medium? So rather than thinking, 'that would never work in my stand-up act,' you might think 'great, there's an article/sketch/cartoon in that, or that would make a great short story.' Comedian and writer Dan Evans says, 'It's about producing stuff, who knows specifically what it'll end up being. I used a line in a short story that was a failed stand-up joke from years before that I stumbled upon in my notebook.'

So even though it's frustrating if you want jokes for a specific thing now, they will usually be part of the overall mix of your joke writing life. So be grateful you've got ideas. Keep all your old notebooks.

Question: Why do I sometimes not see the joke potential for months or years after I wrote it?

Answer: I don't know! It happens to me too. But I do know if you really want to speed things up then you should share your ideas with a friend or a group who understands joke writing philosophy and will go with the flow. There's more about this in Chapter 10, 'Never be ashamed of your joke writing process.' But basically the more brains you have to work on ideas the more chance you have of someone spotting the joke.

Question: I'm a stand-up comic and now I'm getting paid gigs I don't like trying out new material because surely the audience have paid for a good set?

Answer: I know it feels like that but all audiences will cope with one joke that doesn't work, especially if it's not your opening line. And deeper than that they might even love you for it. They know stand-ups have to try jokes out, if you can acknowledge that something doesn't work then you can probably get a laugh out of it. And then the audience will warm to you even more. If I managed to try one new joke out in a 20 minute act it gave me a spring in my step, set my whole routine afire, gave me a bit of excitement that I wasn't going through the same old thing again. Frank Skinner says 'if you're not going forward then you're going backward'. Just doing one new joke per set means you are going somewhere.

Question: What's a good hit rate for new material to work?

Answer: When I was a stand-up I once set myself the task of getting one new joke a week into my act on the basis that by the end of the year I'd have 52 new jokes. My act had roughly three jokes per minute so 60 jokes per 20 minute set. To do this I found I needed to write ten jokes a week, try out three or four and one would stick. I did this religiously for about six months but despite putting a lot of work I didn't achieve my goal. This was partly because some of it was topical so even though I often got more than one new joke a week they were often gone just as fast. Still setting myself that target meant by the end of the year I had about 10 minutes of solid new stuff and a bank of topical jokes that could be adapted at will to each new situation. People started to say I was prolific and it made me laugh if they knew how hard it was.

But that's me, other people are different. I remember being in a dressing room with Dara O'Briain one night and when I told him that I had a new joke to try he said he did too.

And indeed we both did. I went on and did my one joke which of course took 20 seconds. His 'joke' was in fact a new routine, a brilliant comic idea that took him five minutes to expound. He only needed four new 'jokes' to get a new 20 minute act. Yes I was jealous but that's Dara; for the rest of us there's joke writing

SUMMARY

If you've written some jokes but they don't work yet. Stop moaning and start honing!

IS THERE SUCH A THING AS FEAR OF THINKING?

The mind is like a parachute,
it has to be open to work.

FRANK ZAPPA

A comic friend of mine was always complaining that she needed new material. 'I'm getting quite desperate,' she confided to me one day and asked if I could help her.

'Okay, how much time are you spending writing at the moment?' I asked.

'None,' she said, and laughed. 'Maybe that's the problem?'

Yeah, maybe!!!

Even if she spent the amount of time she currently spends complaining about not having any new gags, trying to write, she'd get somewhere.

'But when I sit down to write nothing comes and I get frustrated,' she said.

That in a nutshell is the biggest problem all joke writers face. The first time you sit down to do anything is hard. The ability to accept that and just get on with it is probably the difference between being successful or not. Even though the exercises in this book are designed to get you doing something it's not always as straightforward as that.

When my joke writing classes sit down to do an exercise, I often ask 'who's nervous?'

Most of them are. Yet we're not bungee jumping, not sky diving or mountain climbing. We're sitting in a room with some paper and pens.

What they're probably afraid of is failure, looking silly in front of the group, or realising that they are not as witty as they hoped. But at this stage all we are doing is sitting writing, we haven't got to perform or say it out loud yet, we've just got to do the exercise. So what we're really afraid of is thinking!

When I was a comic I used to dare myself to think about things to walk down a path, to get surreal, to juxtapose two concepts, to go through the motions and at first it was sometimes strangely scary.

Perhaps we are all afraid to walk down an avenue when we don't know the outcome, in life and in joke writing.

But that's what you have to do.

Action may not always bring happiness but there is no happiness without action

BENJAMIN DISRAELI

Joke writing is joke thinking, and joke thinking is going places that are mentally scary and putting your thoughts on the line. Does it matter if you spend 10 minutes going down an avenue and it doesn't work out?

If jokes were that easy to write we wouldn't laugh so hard at them. A joke writing brain is just one step ahead of all the other brains that we want to understand and admire our joke. It can't be outside anyone's grasp, unless you don't understand jokes in the first place.

Jokes are exaggeration, lateral thinking, twisting words, applying one situation to another, taking things out of context, mimicking, slapstick, observation and any combination of the above.

Ideas enlarge the mind, and once the mind has been stretched, it never goes back to its original size.

ROBERT MANKOFF

What's more we all make jokes naturally to a greater or lesser extent. As I said in the foreword I'm trying to mimic and speed up the brain's natural joke writing ability and that means exploring a lot of different avenues, and seeing which ones work and which ones don't. When you tell a joke it looks great that you have walked down an avenue and got to the joke. The listener doesn't know all the avenues you tried where there wasn't a joke. And we don't need to tell them about it we just need to be prepared to walk down those avenues to find jokes.

So each joke writing exercise in this book is a way to walk down an avenue. And walking down an avenue is a metaphor for thinking.

It's not just doing the exercises that's important. It's thinking about them. For example, you could do a double joke-web and might stumble across a link. Unless you think about how to use that link (by exploring different avenues with it) it's just a link on a piece of paper. When you bash two subjects together unless you think each one through you might not create any jokes at all.

I have been accused of making joke writing look easy in my classes and the students find it much harder when they get home. The reason joke writing exercises work in class is the sheer number of brains all going down different avenues, so between us we cover every available base. There are no distractions, there's nothing else to do, they've paid me to make them write jokes so no matter how scared, sceptical or reluctant they are at the beginning, the group energy will carry them along.

I know when some people do the exercises alone their old fears can kick back in and that's partly because it's bound to take more time at home than it does in class because you've got to explore each avenue yourself and you haven't got anyone to make you do it, so it's easy to give up.

If you relax a bit you actually write more than if you're worried about blank pages and so on.

GRAHAM LINEHAN

Believe it or not it works the other way too.

I find it much easier to come up with jokes when I am with a class than when I'm working at home.If I get stuck at home now, I go through the motions of imagining a class. When I take my class through each step I have to practise what I preach, I can't abandon anything, I have to see everything through. And you know what? It works, and the jokes come, some of them even written by the imaginary students themselves!

You can do that too.

Imagine you are with a class, explaining the ideas, walk down each avenue with them, see everything through and see the difference it makes.

I really do understand fear of thinking because sometimes in class even I have felt like that but I can't admit it or indulge it I just have to carry on, going through the exercises exploring each avenue and walking my talk. So if you hit a blank and the fear comes up, you have a choice you can spend your time and energy indulging in the fear or you can carry on working.

SUMMARY

There may be many things to fear in this world. Don't let thinking be one of them.

Why not dare yourself to do one of these joke writing exercises? Really do it, put the time in, think things through, walk down unknown routes and see what happens.

IS THERE SUCH A THING AS FEAR OF THINKING?

CHAPTER FIFTEEN

CASE STUDY

A TRUE ACCOUNT OF WRITING JOKES ON A DIFFICULT SUBJECT ON A DEADLINE (WHILST LOOKING AFTER MY MOTHER)...

THURSDAY AM

Comedienne friend phones. She has to do a big gig to a room full of building site managers being run by a House Building regulations firm.

'Don't fall asleep,' she says as she explains it to me.

She's had their company blurb for a while but hasn't written any jokes. The gig is in one week. Can I help?

'I'm not trying to get out of it but I'm just on my way to my mother's,' I tell her. 'She's had another fall but I'll do what I can.'

I'm thinking I can fit the odd half hours writing around my mother's schedule and keep notes to use as a case study.

I download the company blurb (ten pages in tiny grey text), pack it in my case, make sure I have my glasses (it really is tiny text), put the dog in the car and drive one hundred and forty miles to Dorset.

THURSDAY PM (30 MINS)

I get my mother settled and start looking at the company brochure that I downloaded. I go through their blurb line by line and pick out anything interesting[31]. This should also educate me about their organisation. Basically, at the gig, the housing regulations firm are giving awards to building site managers.

I read their blurb twice and pick out the following...

- Their regulations are the **Bible** of the house building industry.
- They are looking for the **X Factor** in their site managers.
- They are interested in the site managers' **Interpretation** of plans
- and 'the awards are recognised as **Oscars** of the house building industry'

I decide the most interesting word is Bible, so I free associate on it. How will other religions deal with it? I need to be careful not to stray into offending people. I know the comedienne's husband's Jewish and write the line:

These regulations are the Bible of the building industry apparently...

My husband's Jewish; he would only follow half of them.

I think about house building and stone and the 10 commandments being set in stone...

---

[31] As in Writing Jokes From Newspapers (Chapter 7)

If these regulations are the Bible of the house building industry are masons' parts actually set in stone?

These are a start. I'm always pleased when I write something straight away.

I don't yet know how to use the other lines I picked out: X Factor, interpretation and Oscars.

I look at them again for a few minutes and hand them over to my background processor[32]. Then I sit and watch telly with my mother.

FRIDAY MORNING (45 MINS)

I look at it all again. My brain's been working on it overnight and I have a few ideas. Admittedly weak ideas but they're a start.

If they are looking for the X Factor does Simon Cowell come and say the house you just built is rubbish?

Could interpretation be to do with dance?

These awards are very masculine but the Oscars are very camp – how can I get that into a joke?

I have another read through of their blurb; yesterday I noticed that they are a **'non-profit distributing company'** but hadn't highlighted it. Today it seems to jump out at me.

I know a few people who are 'non profit distributing'... Is that a byword for meanness?

---

[32] See Background Processing (Chapter 2)

I decide that the regulations being the 'Bible' of the house building industry is still the most interesting thing and so do a double joke-web[33] pitching building regulations against the Bible. I do two small ones on the back of the blurb I printed out.

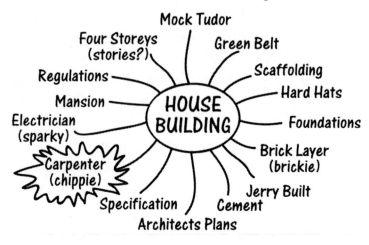

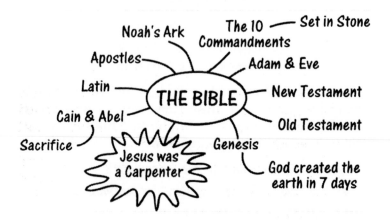

---

[33] See Double Joke-Webs and the Hadron Joke Collider (Chapter 5)

FRIDAY AFTERNOON (30 MINS)

Even though I finished my two joke-webs this morning I didn't get a chance to collide them.

'Carpenter' appears on both joke-webs so I think about that first. Also 'storeys' (as in the number of floors a building has) could be the same as 'stories' in the Bible.

To go deeper into it I apply every association from 'Bible' to 'house building' and think about each one.

Did building regulations apply to Noah's Ark?

Could the Garden of Eden now be The Green Belt?

When God created the universe did he wear a hard hat? Did he stick to the architect's plans?

God had a son who was a carpenter. Did he have a second little-known son who was an electrician?

Did his carpenter son help build the universe?

I feel very pleased to have ideas.

SATURDAY MORNING (20 MINS)

I wasn't going to have any time today as the family are coming to visit but my brother Ken has phoned to say he'll be late so I can do a bit. I feel reluctance, as if there won't be any more jokes, but I know this old feeling, those old blocks and ignore them. I sit in my mum's sunny garden and just get on with it. I work on the planning permission line and come up with:

God created the earth in seven days but only because he didn't have to get planning permission.

I think about the nursery story of the *Three Little Pigs* building houses but don't know where it can fit in.

I do a small joke-web (really a miniature!) on 'awards' which yields nothing until I 'Hadron Joke Collide' the idea of 'awards' against 'building houses'.

Then I come up with...

Optimists in the room have brought in their hod carriers to take awards home.

Hope you're wearing hard hats, you're about to be showered with awards.

(nice lines for giving out awards – not real jokes)

The masons award is actually set in stone.

(reworking of other gag, which is good because it was rubbish in its other form?)

Did God get an award for creating the planet?

I manage to do 20 minutes before my brother arrives. I realise that my initial feeling that there were no more jokes is completely wrong (as usual).

My brother is an electrician. He raises his eyebrows when I tell him I am writing jokes about house building. So I decide to tell him the jokes, weak ones and all.[34] He loves the 'second son of God being an electrician' one and genuinely smiles at the other ones. I feel pleased because he is similar to the audience she'll have.

SATURDAY PM (25 MINS)

I'm sitting in the same room as my mother who is watching *The Weakest Link* and I can't help but look up and answer the odd question.

I realise that the 'God having a second son who was an electrician' stuff might be great for a surrealist comic to riff on but the comic I'm writing for isn't that surreal.

I finally find an angle on the awards being the Oscars of the building industry...

Would the audience of builders be phoning each other up to ask 'who are you wearing?'

Then I wonder whether builders even understand that line? Whatever – I'll give it to the comic and she can decide.

I phone her up from my mother's and give her everything I have so far. She seems thrilled that I have got anything at all. I tell her I'm driving back

---

[34] See Never Be Ashamed of Your Joke Writing Process (Chapter 10)

tomorrow, having the next day running errands and can be on the case again on Tuesday.

MONDAY

The comic texts me to say she's written a joke based on the X Factor line.

I hear they're looking for the X Factor. I hope your careers last longer than the ones on the show.

What a lovely line! It's funnier than the one I thought of. My thinking has clearly sparked her thinking, which often happens once you put some work in[35]. I text her back and tell her it's great.

TUESDAY AM

We're running out of time on this now. I decide to do the Surrealist Inquisition[36] Question Sheet on 'building site inspectors'. I feel a bit daunted so I set myself the target to write for half an hour but then got on a bit of a roll so wrote for 45 minutes.

I start with 'Describe the situation to Aliens. Don't mention any of the key words.'

After a bit of thought I come up with the idea that people who set buildings regulations are Lords of the Dwellings standards (I always imagine what a Star Trek alien would say).

I like the word 'dwellings' it makes me think of mud huts and igloos. I try to imagine what a site inspector would think of mud huts...

---

[35] See What's Most Important: Time, Tenacity or Talent? (Chapter 8)
[36] The Surrealist Inquisition (Chapter 11)

Site inspectors have a terrible time on holiday.

'Oh that mud hut needs better foundations!'

'Look at the state of that igloo!'

Can you imagine them seeing the leaning tower of Pisa, it could ruin the whole holiday.

Then I move onto 'Describe the situation to a young child'.

How could a young child cope with building standards? I think very hard and realise they have their own building disaster fable in the *Three Little Pigs* (which I'd thought about yesterday). I get quite excited about this because I am starting to see how I can use it.

The comedienne I'm writing for has a daughter so it might fit in with other stuff she is doing?

Would the executive from the building company insist their kids read the *Three Little Pigs* story over and over?

I try rewriting the fairy tale so the buildings inspector comes along while the three little pigs are building their houses and makes them build it again so that the wolf goes hungry.

I explained to my daughter that building regulations were introduced after the three little pigs housing disaster...

In the modern version we have the straw house, the brick house and the really stupid house built on a flood plain.

Next I do: 'See if you can find an analogy'.

Do animal dens (rabbits' warrens, birds' nests etc.) have building regulations? And building inspectors? Do birds wolf whistle each other when they are building their nests (because they have become builders)?

And finally: 'Think about it from the point of view of the objects/things/people who are indirectly involved.'

I think of it from the point of view of the land being built on. The animals' houses are displaced so people can have houses... I realise a new homes company is not going to want jokes about that so I stop that train of thought!

TUESDAY PM (15 MINS)

I lock myself in the bedroom and go through everything I've got, saying the lines out loud to an imaginary audience of building site managers[37]. I have to tweak some of them to get the words to flow and I am tempted to abandon a couple of them altogether!

WEDNESDAY AM (1 HOUR)

I decide the final thing is to do a joke-web on 'relationships' to collide against the previous joke-web on 'building regulations'. The comedienne does a lot of relationship stuff and she's got to segue this stuff in with her act.

---

[37] See Honing (Chapter 13)

It's another sunny day so I sit in the garden and do a joke-web about relationships. It's interesting the way the mind works because knowing that I'm going to collide my 'relationships' joke-web against 'building regulations', my mind starts to include things in advance. So when I write 'love songs' I come up with the Oasis song *Wonderwall* which naturally links to buildings. This is obviously not a fluke – I love the way joke writing brains work. I wonder whether building site managers find this song romantic?

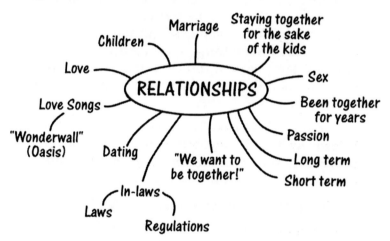

While I am sitting there my partner comes out. I say I am colliding building regulations against relationships. He thinks for a while and comes up with...

> *A building project is like a wife... She always costs more than the original estimate.*

I'm not sure my client will like it, but when I read it to her later that's the joke she likes most – always happens!

I 'Hadron Joke Collide' my subjects and come up with...

Being in a relationship is like being a house builder...

You have annoying laws...

I have annoying in-laws!

It's weak, I know, I'm just trying to show the process here!

I phone the comic up and she likes the pigs stuff and the joke my partner wrote. I tell her I've got one more method of joke writing to run it through - *Stream-of-Consciousness*. Although, I tell her that's ideally something she has an opinion on as I'm not sure how strongly I feel about building regulations. She says she can't learn anymore anyway so not to bother.

I have a lovely break. Then, even though I thought I had switched my brain off, my background processor went on running, and, in the middle of the night, I thought of the joke.

You've got to educate them young. My kid plays with Lego in the lounge, every now and then I run in and shout, 'you can't build there you haven't got planning permission!'

Which is a bit like the God creating the universe one, but I don't know if she's using the God one so I send it off. My work is done!

Adding it up I've spent four and a half hours on a difficult subject. I've used three different joke writing methods and got 12 – 15 ideas. Not all of them worked out but they might have done if I had more time!

SUMMARY

If I can write jokes on house building regulations – then you can write jokes on, well, anything...

CASE STUDY

AFTERWORD: HOW TO MAKE JOKE WRITING FUN

Start early.

Invite someone round to write with you, bribe them with cake if necessary which they can only have after an hour's work.

See who can come up with the most rubbish joke on a subject – let them out joyfully, just to free things up.

Play verbal word games, take whatever subject you have and break up the major words involved in it and try and pun on them. Try this yourself or with a partner (this is a particularly good way of writing bad jokes!)

Start very early.

Think to yourself I am going to open up my mind to joke writing.

Just trust. Jokes are there and you're going to find them. All you have to do is put the time in.

Smile while you work. Whistle so the jokes hiding in the corners of your mind can hear you coming.

Start *really* early.

If you need jokes for Thursday, start writing on Monday then you can sit back and go on an open ended exploration because you have so much time.

Lay on the floor and imagine the subject you are trying to write about being played out on the ceiling.

Go for a mental walk into the unknown and don't worry if you don't find a joke there.

Go for a real walk and gently mull over the subject.

Allow yourself to think the unthinkable like what's the opposite of what you think might happen?

Act a situation out, mime it, mimic it, mine it.

Tell a story and exaggerate wildly.

Breathe, expand your mind outwards and smile inwards.

Relax.

Don't forget to start early now.

BIBLIOGRAPHY

Carr, Jimmy & Greaves, Lucy, *The naked Jape Uncovering the hidden world of jokes* (Penguin books) 2007

Allen, Tony, *Attitude - Wanna Make Something of it?* (Gothic Image Publications) 2002

More Viz Crap Jokes (John Brown Publishing Ltd.) 1999

Murray, Logan, *Be a Great Stand-up* (Hodder) 2010

Robert Leahy, *Anxiety Free: Unravel your fears before they unravel you* (Hay House)

Lamont, Anne, *Bird by Bird: Instructions on Writing and Life* (Anchor Books) 1995

Skinner, Frank, *On The Road: Love, Stand-up Comedy and The Queen of the Night* (Century) 2008

Carter Judy, *Stand-Up Comedy – The Book,* (Bantam, Doubleday, Bell) 1990

Cameron, Julia, *The Artists Way* (Souvenir Press) 1994

Jeffers, Susan, *Feel The Fear and Do It Anyway,* (Arrow Books) 1991

Armstrong, Jesse & Bain, Sam, *Peep Show: the scripts and more* (Transworld) 2008

Bradbury, David & McGrath, Joe, *Now That's funny! Writers on writing comedy* (Methuen) 1998

ABOUT SALLY HOLLOWAY

After eleven years on the comedy circuit Sally Holloway became one of the country's top female comics, gigging in Britain and around the World.

Nowadays, she uses her skills to teach others and has been breaking new ground with her innovative and radical joke writing techniques.

As well as in her own classes she has showcased these ideas on Radio 4's *Word of Mouth*, at the British Society of Comedy Writers' Conferences and the Edinburgh Festival.

AUTHOR PHOTO BY BEA LACEY

For many years she was single and lived in London devoted to her cat, but now she lives in East Sussex with her boyfriend and a dog.

Learn more or book your place on one of Sally's courses at... www.comedycourses.biz

Also available from Bookshaker.com

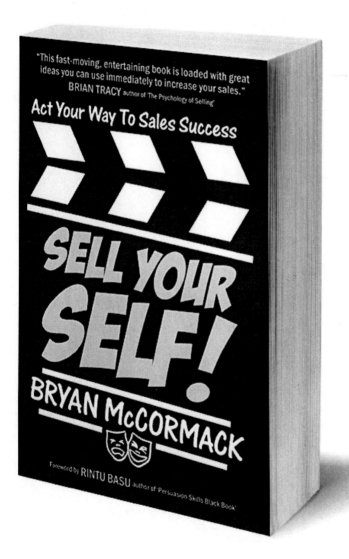

Lightning Source UK Ltd.
Milton Keynes UK
15 March 2011

169287UK00007B/11/P